MW01600899

THE THRIVING COACH

*How To Transform Lives and
Create A Business You Love*

FRANK MACRI

Access Your Free Audiobook

For an even more immersive experience, I invite you to access the free audiobook version of this book.

The audiobook is designed to help you increase your reading speed and retain more information.

Listening to the book allows you to absorb the material during your daily commute, workouts, or any other time you have available, making it a powerful hack to gain even more value.

To download the audiobook, simply scan the QR code below or visit...

vwww.thrivingcoachacademy.com/audiobook

Copyright © 2025 by Frank Macri. All rights reserved.

No part of this book may be reproduced, stored in a retrieval system, or transmitted in any form or by any means—electronic, mechanical, photocopying, recording, or otherwise—without prior written permission from the publisher, except for brief quotations used in reviews or other non-commercial purposes.

This book is a work of nonfiction. The stories, examples, and testimonials included are based on real-life experiences but may have been modified for clarity or illustrative purposes. Any resemblance to actual persons, living or dead, is purely coincidental.

The information provided in this book is for educational and informational purposes only. The testimonials and success stories included are individual experiences and are not guarantees of specific results. Financial outcomes and personal success depend on individual effort, market conditions, and personal circumstances. The author and publisher disclaim all liability in connection with the use of this material.

Self-published by Frank Macri
Raleigh, North Carolina, USA
www.thrivingcoachacademy.com

ISBN: 979-8-89694-046-3 Paperback
ISBN: 979-8-89694-047-0 eBook
ISBN: 979-8-89694-268-9 Hardcover

Printed in the United States of America

For inquiries, please contact:
admissions@thrivingcoachacademy.com

ACKNOWLEDGMENTS

T his book is dedicated to all the incredible students of Thriving Coach Academy.

Your courage, passion, and commitment to making a difference in the lives of others inspire me every single day. Thank you for trusting me to be part of your journey and for pouring your heart into mastering the art of coaching. Each breakthrough you achieve with your clients serves as a powerful reminder of why I began this work and why it matters so much.

To those who have believed in me and this mission—whether you've been part of the Academy from the very beginning or joined along the way—you are the heartbeat of this movement. Your stories, questions, and successes have shaped this book and every lesson within it.

This book is for you. May it serve as a guide, a companion, and a reminder that you are capable of creating the thriving career and life you deserve. Here's to your continued growth and impact.

Together, we are changing lives—one coaching session at a time.

IS THIS BOOK FOR YOU?

Many people wonder if a career in coaching is the right fit for them. Not everyone knows right away whether or not coaching is their calling, but there are often signs and feelings that point them in that direction.

Maybe you're fascinated by psychology. You might be a natural people-person, drawn to understanding and helping others. You want to show people they have the power to shape their own lives. Feeling a strong sense of purpose in your work drives you.

Or perhaps you've realized that your current job, while stable, feels like a means to an end. It doesn't fulfill your deeper purpose. You crave more freedom. Living on your own terms and making your own rules appeals to you. Building something lasting and meaningful is what truly excites you.

Or, deep down, you feel destined for greatness. You've always liked helping people achieve their dreams, connecting with them on a deeper level, and holding space for their thoughts and emotions. Your voice is unique, and you want it to be heard. You're passionate about helping others become the best version of themselves.

These things are likely all true. It's also likely true that right now, you're feeling burned out in your current job. The structure and routine that once provided comfort now feel like chains holding you back. You want to break free and do something that truly matters to you, something that aligns with your passions and values, and something that gives you the freedom and flexibility you crave.

If this resonates with you, then you've picked up the right book. It's designed to guide you on a transformative journey toward becoming a successful and impactful coach. You'll learn how to harness your natural strengths and passions, how to build a lucrative career while providing quality service, and how to create a life that gives you freedom and fulfillment.

This book will serve as your roadmap to turning your calling into a thriving coaching business that makes a real difference in the world. I'll share the most valuable concepts and lessons I've learned from my experiences working in the coaching industry for over a decade.

In the first section of this book, I will share why you already have gifts inside you that can transform lives.

In the second section, you'll see how you can develop a coaching mindset so that you can think like a high-level coach and feel confident in your sessions.

In the third section, we'll discuss how to master the art of coaching, including the secret coaching method that creates fast breakthroughs for clients.

In the fourth section, you will learn the best strategies to grow a profitable coaching business you love.

Finally, in the fifth section, you will discover the best strategies to attract premium clients and make your first million as a coach.

There has never been a better time than now to enter the field of coaching. Congratulations on your decision to purchase this book and explore a career as a professional coach.

Your clients are waiting for you.

CONTENTS

The Wake-Up Call

My heart raced as I sat in the doctor's office, waiting for him to deliver the news. For the last few weeks, I had been experiencing heart palpitations and difficulty sleeping, and I knew something was wrong.

When the doctor finally spoke, his words hit me like a ton of bricks. "Your thyroid levels are dangerously high." His voice was grave. "If we don't get them under control, you could face serious health complications."

I felt my heart sink as the gravity of the situation hit me. My mind raced with thoughts of worst-case scenarios and life-threatening illnesses.

I was only sixteen years old at the time. Up until that point in my life, I did not view myself as a leader. During my teenage years, I did not have many friends and avoided being in the spotlight as much as possible. Whenever I was called upon to speak in class, I experienced intense anxiety. I was not anywhere near as confident or outgoing as my peers.

I was constantly worried about what others thought of me and whether I was good enough. This pressure made it difficult for me to assert myself and speak up, especially in groups or social situations. It was overwhelming, and I often felt like I was on the outside looking in.

I felt the same way sitting there with the doctor.

"What happens if the medication doesn't work?" I asked.

"We may need to explore more serious surgeries and treatments. But let's take it one step at a time. For now, let's focus on getting your thyroid levels under control."

In that moment, fear took hold of me like never before. I felt exposed, as though a thin layer of safety had been peeled away, leaving me vulnerable to something beyond my control. A deep sense of uncertainty sank into me, and I realized that everything I'd taken for granted—my health, my future—was no longer guaranteed.

I underwent extensive testing and monitoring over the next two years, all while trying to keep my anxiety and fear at bay. My normal teenage life was turned upside down. I went from worrying about typical teenage concerns to worrying about my health and future.

Back then, I had this naive belief that life was this long, endless road, stretching out before us, full of health and happiness. But boy, was I wrong. It took that health scare to knock some sense into me, to make me realize just how fragile and fleeting life can be.

One burning question continued to echo through my mind: "How can I create a life that's worth living?" This question forced me to reflect on what truly mattered to me, what I valued most, and what I wanted to achieve in my life.

My health finally stabilized within two years. The medication began to work, gradually bringing my thyroid levels back under control, but I had to undergo regular blood work to monitor my progress closely. While the medical issues were resolved, the whole process was like a wake-up call that invited me to start living with intention.

Armed with a newfound sense of purpose and a healthy dose of determination, I embarked on a quest to figure out what the heck I wanted to do with my life.

Spoiler alert: it wasn't the traditional nine-to-five grind that everyone else seemed to be stuck in.

I knew many people who worked those hours and they were always exhausted, frustrated, and stressed. They were always looking for new ways to make money, even when they were supposed to be retired. It was like they were in a never-ending game of financial whack-a-mole.

Instead of waiting for retirement to roll around, I decided to take matters into my own hands. I was on a mission to find work that didn't feel like work—a career that lit a fire in my belly and ignited a sense of purpose within me. Because let's be real, life's too short for boring desk jobs and soul-sucking meetings. I wanted to live up to my potential, not waste away in a cubicle counting down the minutes until happy hour.

I thought, "What career path would allow me to create my schedule, have uncapped earning potential, and still have a positive impact on others?"

I began reading various blogs and books that explored careers related to mental health and personal growth. That's when I first encountered a term I had never seen before: "Life Coach." I learned that a life coach is a professional who helps people move forward by guiding them to uncover their own wisdom and solutions.

Rather than simply giving advice, life coaches create a supportive environment that encourages clients to clarify their goals, overcome obstacles, and tap into their potential to reach new levels of personal and professional fulfillment.

The idea of helping others grow resonated deeply with me. It felt like a perfect blend of purpose, impact, and independence—exactly what I had been looking for. At that moment, it felt like all the puzzle pieces had fallen together.

I realized that was exactly what I had been looking for. Pursuing a career in coaching aligned with everything I value. I felt like, for the first time, I had found my calling. I knew I wanted to pursue coaching with all my heart.

If it weren't for my health scare, I would not have realized the importance of pursuing your true calling in life. I knew I couldn't let anything stand in my way. Every new day was a gift and I refused to take it for granted.

It's easy to get caught up in the daily grind and forget that we are not guaranteed tomorrow. That's why it's necessary to seize every opportunity to live our lives to the fullest and pursue our dreams. If you have a calling or a passion, don't wait for the perfect timing.

The time to act is now. Don't let anything hold you back from sharing your gifts with the world.

Foundations of Coaching

"Where is the wealthiest place in the world? Do you know? It's not China. It's not Dubai. It's in the graveyard. Because in the graveyard, you will find inventions never invented. Businesses never erected. Songs never sung, books never written. Ideas never nurtured, people never realized because they were scared... to take a risk. Scared like you.

But you want to know something else? You're not in a graveyard, yet. We get one life, and every passing moment, we will never get back again. There is no rewind button in life. This moment is so precious. We have to be here, we have to be in it. We have to make the most of it, we have to live our dreams now. Because they are possible."

— *PRINCE EA*

CHAPTER 1

My Humiliating First Coaching Session

When I first decided to become a life coach, I was full of excitement and enthusiasm. I mean, how hard could it be, right? All I needed to do was read a few books, watch a few videos on YouTube, and *voila!* I'd be a fully fledged coach.

I hunkered down with my books and videos, determined to learn everything I could about psychology, communication skills and effective questioning techniques. Eventually, I felt confident enough to try my hand at coaching. I found someone who was willing to let me give them a free coaching session, and I was off to the races.

The session started out well enough. I had my notes in front of me, my questions at the ready, and a big smile on my face. But, as luck would have it, things quickly went south. I got tongue-tied, stumbled over my words, and made a complete fool of myself.

My client, to her credit, tried to be polite about it. But I could tell she was getting frustrated. I mean, who wouldn't be? Here she was, expecting to get some powerful coaching, and instead, she got me fumbling my way through the session like a toddler learning to walk.

Before the end of the session, she said, "You know what? I think we've had enough for today. Thanks for your time, but I don't think I'll be hiring you as my coach."

I was mortified. But, as they say, every cloud has a silver lining. It was that humiliating experience that made me realize I needed to invest in proper training if I wanted to become a good coach.

I enrolled in a training program that, while solid, lacked business support. I now knew how to coach, but there was still one little problem: I still did not know how to find clients.

Okay, maybe it wasn't that "little" of a problem.

I began doing what I thought you were supposed to do when you become a coach: I made a fancy website with my bio and some information about coaching. It had a nice photo of me, a brief description of what coaching was, and a way for people to email me if they were interested.

But this didn't work. No one reached out. I had my website up for a couple months before deciding it wasn't attracting any clients.

It wasn't until I started connecting with people in person that I realized the importance of human interaction. It was a bit like being a hermit crab for a while. I had to slowly emerge from my shell and start mingling with the outside world. I started going to networking events, which felt intimidating at first but became easier over time.

Once I started asking people if they wanted coaching, I experienced a lot of rejection. In fact, I ended up enrolling zero clients during my first year, which left me feeling discouraged and questioning whether I was cut out for this.

I often wondered if success in coaching was just a matter of luck, having money, or knowing the right people. I assumed those were the essential ingredients for building a thriving business, and since I didn't have any of them, I doubted whether success was even possible for me.

But even without those advantages, I realized I had something far more powerful: commitment. I was committed to making this work and sharing the life-changing power of coaching with the world. I convinced myself to keep going, driven by a sense of purpose and determination.

One day, I signed up for a workshop on public speaking, attended by a small group of professionals and entrepreneurs. While networking, I met a woman who was enthusiastic when I told her I was a coach.

We followed up with each other later that week, and she said the words I had been waiting to hear for so long: "I would like to hire you." Finally, I had found my first paying client. She paid for a bundle of sessions, and I began coaching her for one hour per week.

> *I thought, "If I can have one person pay me to coach them, the sky's the limit. If it's possible with one person, then it's possible with another."*

It turns out, that was true. In the next two years, I made $300,000 with my coaching business. I went from having $0 months to $10,000 months to $50,000 months. It was not long after those first two years that I passed my first million dollars earned through coaching.

There were many benefits to running a coaching business that I didn't know about when I was getting into it. I had freedom over my schedule. I felt more financially secure as a coach than I ever felt when I was working for someone else.

I was able to donate to various causes I cared about. I traveled as often as I wanted. However, the most fulfilling part was seeing my clients have breakthroughs. I was making a great income while also making a positive impact.

As my coaching business grew, people in my network began asking me how I did it. I knew I could send them off to coach training, but then they would be learning from people who had no real-world experience in establishing an actual coaching business. It's like learning about financial literacy from someone who is barely able to pay their own bills.

That's when a brilliant idea came to me. I took all the lessons I wish I had learned from the beginning and began to lay it all out for other aspiring coaches. I knew I could relate to them because, not that long ago, I was starting from exactly where they were.

After mentoring my first batch of students and seeing them have success in launching their own coaching businesses, I decided to formalize the process into an official coach training program. Thus, Thriving Coach Academy was born.

Now, my team and I have had the privilege of training thousands of coaches from all around the world. Over several years, we've refined our curriculum to ensure we've adapted to changes and trends in the coaching industry. We've seen people from all walks of life flourish as coaches.

In the next chapter, you'll discover the five signs that show you were born to be a coach.

CHAPTER 2

The Five Signs You Were Born To Coach

When I was a senior in high school, we were given a career test. After filling out a series of questions, the test would provide you with a list of suitable career options given your responses. These were supposed to be based on your personality, strengths and interests.

Back in the day, nobody knew what a coach was unless it involved a whistle and a clipboard. So instead of hearing, "You'd make a great coach," it was more like, "You'd make a great teacher. Maybe a nurse or a therapist."

But the results I got were even further off. According to the test, I was apparently destined for a career in computer programming—a field that felt completely disconnected from who I was and what I cared about.

It's no surprise that many natural-born coaches end up bouncing around various careers, always feeling like something is missing. If you've ever felt like you're playing a never-ending game of career roulette, fear not. This chapter is here to help you figure out if coaching is the missing puzzle piece to your life.

It is a common misconception that having extensive knowledge, a large following, and a charismatic personality are prerequisites for being a successful coach. Based on my personal experience of mentoring thousands of coaches, there are actually five distinct signs that indicate someone is naturally inclined to be a coach.

Sign #1:
You are passionate about making a difference in people's lives.

You find joy in seeing people achieve their goals and dreams, seeing people win, and supporting others in becoming the best version of who they are. If you look at the jobs you've had thus far, you found the most meaning at times when you directly supported others.

Before I became a coach, I had a short-term job as a receptionist at a nutrition school. At first, I thought it would all be about kale, quinoa, and chia seeds, but I quickly realized it was mostly about crunching numbers and typing on a keyboard.

The part of the job that was most fulfilling were the brief moments in the day where I talked with potential students. I loved answering their questions, hearing about their goals, and supporting them in moving forward.

Little did I know that even though my job title was "receptionist," there was actually some coaching involved in the role. That's not uncommon. Many people work various roles—HR, teachers, nurses, therapists, hospitality professionals, sales and marketing professionals—that include some hints of coaching that make them feel meaningful.

Imagine what it would be like to strip away all the things you don't like and focus solely on the parts you enjoy. As a coach, that's what you'd be doing. You would get a front-row seat to the greatest show on earth: your clients' transformation.

Sign #2:
You are naturally curious about people.

You're someone who likes to ask people questions, discover what lights them up, and learn how they see the world. You might find it easy to connect with people and are drawn to understanding them. You probably enjoy some innocent people-watching, too. You sincerely like observing what makes people tick. You prefer deep conversations over small talk.

As we get older, our curiosity can be suppressed and judged. You may have been told to "stop asking so many questions" or "quit being so nosy" as you progressed out of childhood. However, your natural curiosity about people is a gift that can help you ask deep and eye-opening questions as a coach.

As a coach, you get paid well to ask people questions about themselves. Your natural curiosity about people is something that is more rare and valuable than you may realize. If you find that you are intrigued by people, that is a sign you were born to be a coach.

Sign #3:
You believe in people's ability to thrive, no matter the circumstance.

This belief in human potential is a cornerstone of effective coaching. Coaches are adept at seeing beyond the immediate struggles of a situation and recognizing the opportunity in every challenge. You understand that every setback holds the potential for a comeback.

You recognize that we live in a world where every experience, whether pleasant or painful, can offer us valuable lessons. If it feels good, it's here to support us. If it doesn't feel good, it's here to help us grow. While not everything may seem positive at first glance, each experience can be a gift that contributes to our personal growth and resilience.

Coaches support their clients in discovering valuable lessons and growth within challenges. This does not mean we can't have low moments in life. It's normal to have times when you are frustrated, afraid, anxious, and doubtful. You don't have to force yourself to be positive all the time. Even when things get dark, you know that there's a way out.

Believing in possibility is not about minimizing hardship or denying pain. It's about showing up as the hero of your story, rather than the victim. Embracing this mindset empowers you and your clients to navigate life's challenges with courage and confidence. This unwavering belief in the ability of people to thrive, no matter the circumstance, is a sign that you will make a powerful coach.

Sign #4:
People easily open up to you.

One of our graduates, Christopher, spent many years working as a hairstylist. When he was enrolled in our program, he told me how his clients would have deep conversations with him while getting their hair done. He found himself wanting to put the scissors down and simply listen to them as they opened up.

In a world where people often feel judged, providing someone with the space to share their fears, goals, and dreams without judgment can be life-changing. Christopher realized this was a sign he was born to coach and ended up earning $10,000 in his first few months of business.

Coaches listen with the intent to understand someone so they truly feel heard. It's just as important to listen to what someone is saying as it is to listen to what they are not saying. In other words, good coaches pick up on body language, tone changes, and unspoken beliefs that may be holding someone back.

In Thriving Coach Academy, we call these limiting beliefs Old Rules. In Section II of this book, I will share the Rulebook

Coaching Method™ that will cause your clients to have breakthroughs in your coaching sessions.

Sign #5:
You value personal growth.

When you go into a bookstore, you're making a beeline to the "self help" section. While most people are getting lost in romance novels or sci-fi epics, you're diving headfirst into the world of personal growth like it's a buffet of wisdom waiting to be devoured.

In a world where many people are content to simply coast through life without ever challenging themselves, having a thirst for knowledge and a drive for self-improvement is a rare and valuable trait.

If there's one reason we are on this planet, it's to grow. As a species, we are designed to evolve, adapt and innovate. The time, money, and energy that you invest in your growth is always worth it. Don't be afraid to wear your passion for growth proudly. After all, embracing your journey of self-discovery is a sign of strength, not weakness.

Those are the five signs that you were born to coach. How many of these signs do you see in yourself? If you notice most of these signs in yourself, then the potential is undoubtedly there. With the proper knowledge, mentorship, and community, you will undoubtedly flourish as a coach.

Having these signs means there is a gift inside you that is meant to be shared with others. It shows that you were born to transform lives as a professional coach. But before we move forward, let's distinguish how coaching differs from therapy.

CHAPTER 3

Coaching vs. Therapy

To become a successful coach, it's crucial to have a clear understanding of what coaching is and what it's not. The most pivotal distinction is the line drawn between coaching and therapy. Coaching is not better nor worse than therapy; rather, they are two different modalities both designed to support people.

Most therapeutic techniques are designed to support individuals who are going through significant emotional distress. Therapy is ideal for someone suffering from depression, addiction or trauma. One simple way to remember this is the phrase: "Don't Coach D.A.T.!"

The overarching question that therapy explores is, "How can I heal from the past so I can function in the present?" The focus is on resolving parts of someone's childhood and healing from traumatic experiences.

The overarching question coaching explores is, "How can I use my strengths and gifts in the present to create my desired future?" The focus is on bridging the gap between where you are now and where you want to be.

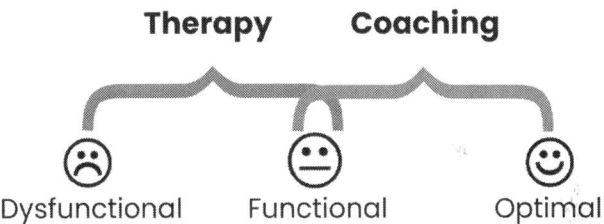

Therapy   Coaching

Dysfunctional   Functional   Optimal

Coaching is ideal for people looking to break through the barriers holding them back from living to their potential. There are many successful people who are stuck, unable to achieve certain goals, but who don't require a therapist to help them process parts of their childhood. Coaching is still transformative and deep, even though it does not address mental dysfunction.

There is some overlap in what kinds of support both a therapist and a coach can address. For example, a well-trained coach can support clients struggling with anxiety, overwhelm, and other challenging emotions.

Therapy	Coaching
Takes someone from dysfunctional to functional	Takes someone from functional to optimal
Focuses on how the past impacts the present	Takes clients from the present to the future
Devotes time to processing your pain	Devotes time to uncovering your strengths
The ultimate result is healing	The ultimate result is flourishing

Process vs. Results

Therapy is process-oriented. The majority of a therapist's work will be on processing a client's feelings, traumas, and childhood. Coaching is results-oriented. People work with coaches to get a specific result or outcome. When you leave a therapy session, you are ready to feel differently. When you leave a coaching session, you are ready to act differently.

Let's say there's an executive struggling to manage her team. The executive probably wouldn't need to explore childhood trauma to improve her management skills. A coach would be an amazing resource to help this executive explore approaches she can take to engage their team.

Now, consider someone who has recently gone through a significant loss and is experiencing intense grief. A therapist would be the appropriate professional to help them process their emotions, work through the stages of grief, and begin healing.

The Right Fit

Sometimes, it's not the problem that dictates the ideal type of support—it's how the person is experiencing the problem. The key indicator is whether the person is mainly looking to resolve the pain they're going through or take steps to move forward.

For example, Person A goes through a breakup with a significant other. After their breakup, they spiral into depression and find it hard to get out of bed in the morning. They would be a great fit for therapy.

Now, let's say Person B also goes through a breakup, but they're in a different headspace. They are ready to move forward, put themselves back into the dating scene, and find lasting love. They would be a fit to work with a relationship coach.

In order to become a therapist in many countries, you must have a master's degree level of education and undergo thousands of hours of field training. When you receive your license, you are only eligible to offer therapy services in the state or province you are licensed in. Professional coaches have total freedom to work with clients from around the world.

One of our graduates, Gayle, makes a great example of this. Gayle worked for decades as a Licensed Marriage and Family Therapist in California. Before she pursued coach training, she could only provide therapy services to clients within California. She felt restricted by these regulations and wanted to impact a more diverse range of clients and transform lives on a broader scale.

Within the first year of earning her coach certification, she expanded her practice and tripled her income.

While the coaching industry is not regulated at the government level, there are governing bodies that define and enforce ethics and professionalism in our field. The most well-known and globally recognized governing body in the industry is the International Coach Federation (ICF). The ICF does not train coaches; however, they provide accreditation to coach training programs (like Thriving Coach Academy) to make sure they are teaching ethical and holistic practices.

Some therapists find employment at mental health facilities or schools that are seeking licensed counselors. Others establish their own private practice to work with clients in the state they are licensed in. If you are more comfortable working for someone else or plan to reside in one location, this can be a great fit.

However, if you have an entrepreneurial spirit and crave more flexibility, coaching might be ideal for you. Coaching offers the freedom to be your own boss, the ability to create diverse programs, and the opportunity to work with clients from anywhere in the world, making it a more location-independent career.

Whether you're drawn to therapy or coaching, both paths offer deeply rewarding opportunities to make a positive difference in people's lives. Whether it's helping someone heal from the past or guiding them toward a brighter future, the chance to be part of someone's journey to growth and fulfillment is a privilege.

CHAPTER 4

Pure vs. Hybrid Coaching

When I began my career as a coach, I was in my early twenties. I had a passion for helping others but lacked extensive life experience in some of the areas I wanted to coach. For instance, I wanted to help clients with relationships and parenting, even though I wasn't married and didn't have kids at the time. One of my biggest concerns was my age. The big question that haunted me was: *do I need to have done the thing my client wants to do in order to coach them?*

You may similarly wonder, do I need to have built a successful business to coach entrepreneurs? Or have overcome major health challenges to coach clients on fitness? Or, as a relationship coach, do I need to have been in a long-term relationship to help clients with theirs?

The answer is: no.

This would be like asking if your doctor has to be in perfect health to treat you. They don't. Doctors are trained to understand the science of the human body, and they rely on their medical expertise—not their personal gym routine—to help patients. The same is true in coaching.

> **You don't need to have all the lived experiences your clients have; you just need the coaching tools that will help them move forward.**

Consider Bob Bowman, the coach of Michael Phelps, who you might know as the most decorated Olympian of all time. Bob Bowman was never an Olympian, but Phelps credits Bowman with being instrumental in his career—he was Phelps's coach from the age of eleven through multiple Olympic victories. Bowman didn't rely on having been in the pool himself; he relied on his knowledge of training techniques, psychology, and strategy to coach Phelps to greatness.

When it comes to coaching, there are two main roads you can take: **Pure Coaching** or **Hybrid Coaching.** Whether you're leading from behind or sharing from experience, both methods work—if you know how to navigate them.

Pure Coaching: Trusting the Client's Inner Wisdom

Let's start with Pure Coaching. Think of Pure Coaching like this: you're the mirror, not the painter. The client holds the brush, creating their own masterpiece, while you reflect back what they see, helping them notice details and perspectives they might have missed.

Pure Coaching is about trusting the client to uncover their own answers. It's based on the belief that they have all the solutions inside them, and your job is to ask powerful questions that lead them toward those answers.

Your Focus:

- Asking thought-provoking, open-ended questions.
- Listening deeply and reflecting back what you hear.
- Encouraging the client to find their own solutions.

An Example of Pure Coaching in Action:

Imagine you're working with a client who wants to start a business. Instead of offering your own advice on how to get started, you'd ask questions like:

- What does success look like for you, a year from now?
- What's the deeper reason you want to start this business?
- What do you feel is currently holding you back?

You're not sharing your own stories of how you started a business, or giving them a playbook. You're allowing them to come to their own conclusions.

Pure Coaching Is Right for You If...

- You believe in the power of self-discovery and client autonomy.
- You want to keep your coaching sessions 100 percent client-centered.
- You're comfortable letting go of giving advice and trusting the client's wisdom.

Pure Coaching might be ideal if you don't have extensive life experience in certain areas. It lets clients focus on their own journey without comparing it to yours.

In Pure Coaching, it's all about *them*. You're not the hero of their story; they are. The coach isn't there to dish out solutions but to guide clients toward their own insights.

Hybrid Coaching: The Art of Sharing Without Steering

If Pure Coaching is all about guiding from behind, Hybrid Coaching is about stepping in and sharing your experiences when it's helpful. Think of Hybrid Coaching as a blend of coaching, consulting, and mentorship. You're still asking powerful questions and giving clients space to think, but you're also drawing from your own life and career to offer relevant insights.

In Hybrid Coaching, your own wisdom and stories come into play, but always with the client's needs front and center. It's a delicate balance between sharing your experiences and ensuring you don't overshadow the client's journey.

Your Focus:

- Sharing personal stories or insights that provide perspective.
- Offering advice when it feels helpful.
- Balancing asking questions with giving direct input.

An Example of Hybrid Coaching in Action:

Imagine you're working with a client who's trying to grow their business but feels stuck. Along with asking them about their challenges, you might say:

- "I've faced something similar in my own business. Would you like to hear how I handled it?"
- "Here's a framework I used when I felt stuck—do you think this could help?"
- "This is what worked for me. How does this resonate with what you're experiencing?"

By offering your own insights, you provide another layer of value, giving the client both the benefit of your experience and the space to adapt it to their own journey.

Hybrid Coaching Is Right for You If...

- You have personal or professional experience that's relevant to your clients.
- You want to blend coaching with mentorship or consulting.
- You're comfortable balancing listening with offering advice when needed.

Hybrid Coaching shines when you have personal achievements that clients find inspiring. Your success becomes a powerful motivator for them to push forward. Clients see you as a living, breathing example that what they want to achieve is possible.

However, this approach also comes with a warning: your success may be a great story, but it's not the *only* story. One of the pitfalls of Hybrid Coaching is the temptation to project your path onto your clients. What worked for you might not work for them, and you could end up steering them toward solutions that fit your experience rather than theirs.

Coaching Isn't One-Size-Fits-All

At its core, Pure Coaching is about the client discovering their own path, while Hybrid Coaching allows you to share your own experiences to help guide them. But it's important to remember that coaching isn't a one-size-fits-all approach. Whether you stick to Pure Coaching, lean into Hybrid Coaching, or mix both, your adaptability to the client in front of you is what makes you truly effective—not your résumé, life experience, or accolades.

When I started coaching in my early twenties, I didn't have much life experience to share. I hadn't built a multi-million-dollar business, and I hadn't achieved extraordinary milestones. What I did have was the ability to listen and ask the right questions. I focused on Pure Coaching, and what I quickly discovered was that clients were having incredible breakthroughs—not because of my advice or guidance, but because those insights came from within them.

It was a powerful realization: I didn't need to have the same results my clients were chasing in order to help them achieve success. I needed to trust the coaching process and my clients' ability to find their own answers. The success they had was their own, and I was just there to hold the space and help facilitate their journey.

So, whether you're just starting out or you've got years of experience under your belt, you should remember that you don't need to have climbed the mountain to help someone reach the top. You just need the tools, the questions, and the belief in your client's ability to make the climb on their own terms.

CHAPTER 5

Why People Hire Coaches

I was the biggest skeptic of life coaches before I decided to become one. Before I started my coaching business, I went online and looked up professional coaches to get a better sense for the industry. I found one named Alicia, whose website immediately caught my eye—she seemed very approachable, had numerous client success stories, and had been working as a coach for many years.

Intrigued, I sent her a message saying, "Hey, I noticed you work as a coach, and I'm thinking about exploring a career in coaching. I have some questions on what it takes to be a successful coach and why people hire coaches. Would you be open to grabbing coffee sometime?"

She was quick to respond and invited me to stop by her office in downtown Vancouver. I'd seen countless ads and testimonials online, but part of me wondered if it was all just a sales pitch—did life coaching really make a difference, or was it simply a trend that people latched onto when they felt lost?

As I sat across from Alicia in her bright, inviting office, I felt a mix of excitement and doubt. My first question was, "I don't want to sound nuts, but do people actually take you seriously when you tell them you're a life coach?"

She chuckled and said, "Every coach needs formal training if they want to be taken seriously. I didn't start a coaching business without professional mentorship. I went through a training program that taught me how to properly coach. It puts your potential clients at ease when they know they aren't hiring a random person with no credentials.

"Once you start accumulating some client success stories," she continued, "even more people will show interest in working with you. Success stories not only demonstrate your capabilities, but build your credibility as a coach. When potential clients see that you've helped others achieve their goals, it creates a powerful incentive for them to reach out. It's a ripple effect—each client you help paves the way for more clients."

I nodded, absorbing her words. "That makes sense. It's about having the right training while also showing real results."

"Exactly," Alicia replied. "And remember, every successful coach started where you are now: curious and eager to learn."

Feeling reassured, I decided to dig deeper. "This may seem odd to ask, but why do people even hire professional coaches?"

Here are the five reasons she shared:

1. **They're feeling stuck in an area of life and navigating a transition.**
   A coach can provide the necessary support and guidance to help them move forward. This could involve gaining clarity on their priorities, overcoming limiting beliefs, or creating a clear plan of action to achieve their desired outcomes.

2. **They have an incomplete goal and want to make faster progress.**
   People often know what they want to achieve, but struggle to take consistent action. Coaches help clients stay on track by providing the support and accountability they need to follow through.

3. **They are faced with a big decision that they're unsure about.**
   When individuals weigh different options and fear making a regrettable choice, a coach can offer perspective and support to navigate these decisions effectively.

4. **They want to take their life to the next level.**
   Many seek coaching to bring more passion and excitement into their lives, aiming to make their experiences more meaningful and fulfilling.

5. **They've tried several things, but haven't achieved the desired results.**
    Clients often feel frustrated after attempting various solutions without success. Coaches help identify new strategies and approaches tailored to the individual's needs.

"I love my clients. People who hire coaches are generally goal-oriented, ambitious, and self-aware," she added.

"I'm sure it's fulfilling to work with enjoyable clients," I said. Then, I felt my inner skeptic start to come out again. "It all sounds wonderful, but is coaching just trendy right now? Is there really that much of a demand for it?"

"That's a great question. Frankly, the demand for coaching has experienced a notable increase and continues to look promising," she said. "As long as there are people who are willing to grow, there will be people who want to be coached."

Here are the four reasons she shared as to why interest in coaching has likely increased in recent years:

1. **Rising Awareness of Mental Health and Well-being.**
    More people are recognizing the importance of taking care of their mental and emotional health, leading them to seek support and guidance from professionals like life coaches.

2. **High Levels of Stress and Burnout.**
    Modern life is often fast-paced and stressful, leading to high levels of stress, burnout, and dissatisfaction. As a result, individuals are turning to life coaches to help them navigate these challenges, find balance, and achieve greater fulfillment in their personal and professional lives.

3. **Desire for Personal Development and Growth.**
Many individuals are seeking ways to unlock their full potential, set meaningful goals, and lead a life of purpose. Life coaches provide the tools, strategies, and support needed to facilitate this growth and development.

4. **Increased Visibility and Accessibility of Coaching Services.**
The internet and social media have played a significant role in increasing the visibility and accessibility of coaching services. Individuals can now easily find and connect with coaches online, making it simpler to access the support and guidance they need to improve their lives.

As I left her office, I felt relieved—but still wanted to do my own research. One study I found was from the International Coaching Federation (ICF), which created the Global Coaching Study—the largest global assessment of the state of the coaching profession.

The ICF reported a 60 percent increase in total annual revenue for the coaching industry from 2019 to 2022, reaching $4.564 billion. Additionally, around 80 percent of coaches in this study expressed that their clients expect coaches to be certified or credentialed.

With the evidence piling up—from meeting a successful coach to discovering data on coaching's growth—I realized I could no longer cling to my uncertainty. Holding onto doubt forever only keeps you standing still. It was time to stop being skeptical and start seeing the possibilities. The potential coaching presented was too compelling to overlook.

Regardless of the outcome, I was certain that this journey would be nothing short of an extraordinary adventure.

Understanding why people hire coaches made me realize the profound impact I could have, and it fueled my excitement to dive into this rewarding profession.

Now, it's your turn to imagine the possibilities. Here are some questions to reflect on as you continue through the rest of this book:

What if there are people out there eager to hire you as their coach?

What if your coaching aspirations take off beyond your wildest imagination?

What if you could actually make a living doing something you are passionate about?

What if you could inspire and transform lives all over the world?

What if this new path brings you fulfillment and joy every single day?

It all starts with you allowing your dreams to be possible.

Footnote:

1. International Coaching Federation, "Professional Coaching Continues Global Expansion," ICF Blog, accessed November 5, 2024, https://coachingfederation.org/blog/professional-coaching-continues-global-expansion.

CHAPTER 6

"No Big Deal" Bias

Years ago, I was mentoring a student who struggled to identify the niche she wanted to pursue for her coaching business. She believed her life was rather ordinary because she hadn't accomplished anything extraordinary.

I encouraged her to share more about the defining moments she had experienced. She immediately began discussing her relationship. A few years after going through a difficult divorce, she fell in love with a new man, and they were now happily together.

She said, "I met my now-husband online through a dating app. He was drawn to my dating profile. As we chatted more, we formed a quick connection. It's no big deal really..."

"Stop right there," I interjected. "Do you realize how extraordinary that is?"

She blinked, clearly taken aback. "Well, it was just an online profile."

"Exactly!" I replied with a grin. "You've cracked the code to online dating without even breaking a sweat. While others are swiping left and right in desperation, you've found your happily ever after with a mere tap of the screen. That's like discovering a unicorn in your backyard and thinking it's just a stray horse!"

Her eyes widened with realization, and a spark of excitement ignited within her. "Maybe it is a big deal," she mused, her mind clearly racing with possibilities. Suddenly, she recognized she could make a significant difference helping people find love through online dating.

This pattern is something I've observed in many coaches I've mentored. I call it the No Big Deal Bias. This bias manifests in two key ways:

1. You discredit the things that come naturally to you that other people struggle with.
2. You minimize a major accomplishment after you achieve it.

I believe there is a six-figure coaching business inside every person drawn to this work. The key is to recognize the value you possess right now. Most gifted individuals are blissfully unaware of their own brilliance.

Another coach I mentored was also exploring avenues down which to take her coaching business. She wanted to support clients facing various health challenges but couldn't pinpoint the exact direction to go. Interestingly, she hadn't experienced any major health transformations in her own life.

On the day we were chatting, I was a bit tired because I had not slept well the night before.

"I wish I had an off switch for my brain at night when I am lying in bed. Do you ever wish that?" I asked.

She smiled and replied, "Not really. I'm one of those people who can fall asleep the moment my head hits the pillow."

I raised an eyebrow. "Wait—do you know how rare that is? Many people would pay good money to be able to do that!"

She laughed, shaking her head. "I never thought of it as a skill. It's just how I've always been."

"That's the beauty of it," I said. "You don't even think about it, but for someone else, it could be the solution they've been searching for. What if you could coach people to get the same kind of restful nights that come naturally to you?"

She hesitated. "I don't know… Would people really need a coach for something like that?"

I nodded. "Absolutely. Think about how many people lie awake for hours, unable to sleep. If you can coach them to improve their sleep, you'd be changing their lives. It doesn't have to be complicated—just sharing what you already do naturally could make a massive impact."

The idea started to sink in. "I guess I never thought about it like that," she said.

What she once thought of as "no big deal" became the foundation of a full-time coaching business, helping others find the restful sleep they had been craving.

If something comes naturally to you, you may find it odd to make a living supporting others through it. After all, when something feels effortless, we often underestimate its value or dismiss the idea of turning it into a profession. This is particularly true in a culture that glorifies struggle and hardship as prerequisites for success.

We are taught to believe that if something doesn't require immense effort, it can't possibly be valuable. Yet, it's crucial to understand that your innate abilities hold tremendous potential for creating meaningful change in the world.

Imagine if your success as a coach could flow naturally from the strengths and abilities you already possess.

The No Big Deal Bias teaches two powerful lessons about creating a successful coaching business. First, you can take seemingly simple achievements or outcomes in your own life and turn them into a profitable business.

What feels routine or easy to you could be exactly what someone else needs help with. Your natural strengths and experiences hold immense value.

Second, you don't need to help people with extraordinary challenges to make an impact. Coaching isn't necessarily about solving life's biggest problems—it's about helping clients optimize specific areas of their lives. Even small improvements, like establishing a productive morning routine or gaining confidence in social situations, can have a profound ripple effect. These "simple" shifts can transform someone's life in ways they never imagined.

Here are some examples of things in life we might consider No Big Deal, but can potentially evolve into profitable coaching niches:

- Having a productive morning routine.
- Ending a relationship or marriage.
- Asking people out on dates.
- Being in a happy relationship or marriage.
- Raising well-adjusted children.
- Moving to a new city or country.
- Living in a clutter-free home.
- Posting engaging content online.
- Starting a side hustle.
- Crafting an effective résumé.
- Interviewing with confidence.
- Navigating a career transition.
- Losing weight and maintaining a healthy lifestyle.
- Managing a chronic illness or condition.
- Any form of public speaking or storytelling.
- Learning to speak another language.
- Learning to play an instrument.
- Managing or reducing debt.
- Maintaining a high credit score.
- Setting up retirement funds or investments.
- Achieving an athletic accomplishment.

- Setting and maintaining personal boundaries.
- Managing time effectively.
- Planning a successful event or party.
- Caring for pets or training animals.

These areas can all blossom into a profitable coaching specialty. And this list is by no means exhaustive. It's merely a glimpse into the endless possibilities available to you. You don't need to have lived an extraordinary life to make an extraordinary impact as a coach.

Maybe you're the friend everyone turns to for relationship advice, or perhaps you have a unique ability to help others feel at ease in social situations. It could be that you have a knack for helping others find their style or navigate personal finance. Whatever it is, don't underestimate its potential.

Any kind of life transition or improvement you've gone through counts. What you think is not a big deal to you can be a huge deal to many others. Don't shy away from what comes naturally to you. What may seem insignificant to you could be the very thing that changes someone else's life. Your idea of No Big Deal could be the start of something truly remarkable.

CHAPTER 7

Who Do You Think You Are?

I once attended a leadership workshop and felt completely out of place. As I walked into the room, I couldn't help but notice how everyone else seemed so polished and put together. They were dressed in sharp suits and chic outfits, exuding an air of confidence that made me feel like I didn't belong. My heart sank as I found a seat, wondering if I had made a mistake by coming.

The facilitator began the workshop with an unexpected exercise. She asked us to take out a piece of paper and write down our biggest insecurity about ourselves—something we believed made us inadequate. I hesitated, my mind racing through a myriad of self-doubts. After a while, I wrote down, "not interesting enough."

The facilitator then invited us to stand up and walk around the room, networking with each other, but with a twist: we had to hold our piece of paper in front of our chests for all to see. My stomach churned at the thought. I was terrified to reveal my deepest insecurity to a room full of strangers who seemed so self-assured.

As I reluctantly walked around the room, I was astonished by what I saw. Every person, no matter how confident they appeared, had something written on their paper. "Not smart enough," "Not attractive enough," "Not experienced enough." All the people whom I had assumed had their lives together were battling their own fears and doubts.

This experience forever changed how I viewed my self-doubts. It taught me that everyone has insecurities, no matter how composed they seem on the outside. The people you admire most still wrestle with insecurities and fears.

It is normal to have self-doubt, especially when you pursue opportunities that invite you to step outside your comfort zone. In psychology, having recurring thoughts of inadequacy is referred to as Impostor Syndrome.

Impostor Syndrome Is Not...	Impostor Syndrome Is...
A flaw about your character	A feature of being a human
Indicative of any deficiency within you	A natural consequence that occurs when anyone strives for excellence
A reflection of your capabilities	A testament to your ambition and drive

As an aspiring coach, you might wonder if you're truly capable of guiding others when you're still navigating your own journey. Here are the three most common concerns aspiring coaches grapple with—and how you can reframe them to unlock your full potential:

1. Who am I to coach others when I'm not yet an expert in coaching?

When I graduated from college, I decided to move to China for two years and work as an English teacher. Each English teacher was assigned a subject to teach in English, such as science, literature, or math. A few days before the start of class, my boss told me that I was responsible for teaching US History to the eleventh and twelfth grade students.

Immediately, I felt my body tighten. US History was always a tough subject for me. How was I supposed to teach it, when I was far from an expert myself?

With sweaty palms and a racing heart, I spent countless hours reviewing the textbook and crafting lesson plans. As the first day of class arrived, I stood before my students, nerves tingling, fearing they might see right through me.

As I was teaching, a student raised his hand. I called on him, bracing for a question I might not have the answer to. To my surprise, his question aligned perfectly with the lesson I had prepared. The rest of Lesson One unfolded seamlessly, leaving me with a sense of relief. I went off to read Chapter Two, which I would teach the following week.

From that experience, I learned a valuable lesson:

You only need to be one chapter ahead of the people you want to serve.

Just one. When it comes to offering value as a coach, you don't need to have all the answers. You simply need to be one chapter ahead.

This concept is the reason over 50 percent of our students in Thriving Coach Academy begin working with paying clients within just a few months of training. Even with only the knowledge of core coaching tools, you can make a meaningful impact.

One of my mentors put it this way: if you know how to give a good back massage, but you don't know how to massage other parts of the body, there are still people who will be grateful to be getting a back massage.

Let's address the next concern:

2. **Who am I to coach others when there are others with more experience than me?**

One time, I was mentoring a coach who struggled to put herself out there.

"I wonder why would anyone choose me as their coach," she shared. "I'm not nearly as talented or experienced as other coaches I admire. I don't see how I can compete in the industry."

I posed a question: "Would you say there are coaches and mentors out there with more experience than me?"

"Yes, I would say so," she affirmed.

"So, what drew you to invest in my coaching?" I inquired further.

Without hesitation, she replied, "It was your energy and your story."

"Exactly." I nodded. "So, if experience wasn't the deciding factor for you, why do you think it has to be for the people you want to coach?

A sense of relief washed over her as the realization dawned.

There will always be individuals with more experience. However, your essence is something no one can replicate. It is unique to you. It's like an undiscovered treasure waiting to be unearthed.

Think of your essence like the vibe you give off. It simply exudes from you, naturally. Perhaps your vibe is gentle and encouraging, or maybe it's fiery and passionate. Either way, there are people out there who will be drawn to your authenticity. Just as in dating, you are someone's "type", regardless of what others bring to the table.

No one can truly be "ahead" of you. They may have more experience, but they're not inherently superior. You're all playing the same game, navigating the same arena. There's space for everyone to thrive.

The coaching industry is diverse. Rather than viewing it as competition, think of it as a community where all can become successful. Every coach has a unique perspective and approach that resonates with different people. Your unique experiences, personality, and insights will attract clients who are specifically looking for what you offer.

You have clients that are already waiting for you. When you share your voice, they will find you.

Finally, let's address the last concern:

3. **Who am I to coach others when I still have problems in my own life?**

Consider this: every professional you admire and seek guidance from also grapples with their own challenges and insecurities. No one has life completely figured out.

Your doctor battles their own health issues, your therapist wrestles with their own anxiety, and your mentors have their own struggles.

There's no prerequisite for having a perfect life to become a coach. You can be a work in progress and still make a tremendous impact in people's lives.

We all carry moments of regret and mistakes from our past. You may have stumbled through a divorce, faced parenting challenges, or made decisions you now question. But here's the truth: at any given moment, we're all doing the best we can with the values, needs, and rules guiding us at that time in our lives.

Instead of letting your past haunt you, leverage it as a source of growth. Focus on the lessons, insights, and strengths your experiences have gifted you. By finding purpose in every experience, you'll release the judgment weighing on your mind.

When a potential client encounters you today, they're not meeting the person you were in the past. They're meeting the version of you that you choose to present—a culmination of your growth, wisdom, and resilience.

> *Your own journey through life's ups and downs gives you a unique perspective and empathy that can deeply resonate with your clients. Your struggles are not barriers to coaching; they are bridges to understanding and connection.*

Clients seek coaches who can relate to their experiences, understand their challenges, and guide them with empathy and wisdom. Your authenticity, forged through your own life experiences, can serve as one of your greatest assets as a coach.

Remember, coaching is not about having all the answers or being perfect. It's about being present, curious, and committed to supporting others on their journeys. Your clients aren't expecting perfection—they're seeking understanding, non-judgment, and encouragement, qualities that you already possess.

In the next section, we'll move beyond the basics and dive into embodying the coaching mindset. You'll discover how to honor a coaching arc, see your clients as heroes, and help them envision a future self that drives their growth.

TOP 10 INSIGHTS

1. Therapy helps people move from dysfunctional to functional, while coaching takes them from functional to optimal.

2. You can choose the coaching style that suits you—guiding clients to find their own answers (Pure Coaching) or sharing your experiences when helpful (Hybrid Coaching).

3. Coaching is a rapidly growing profession with rising demand, as people hire coaches to achieve goals faster, elevate their lives, and overcome obstacles.

4. What feels simple or effortless to you could be exactly what others need, and this can be the foundation of a profitable coaching niche.

5. You don't need to address extraordinary challenges with clients to make a meaningful impact.

6. Feeling inadequate is natural when striving for excellence—it's part of the process, and it doesn't disqualify you from being a great coach.

7. You only need to be one chapter ahead of the people you wish to serve.

8. Your unique essence will attract clients, regardless of your experience.

9. You don't need to have everything figured out before starting your coaching career.

10. Coaching is not about having all the answers, but being present, curious, and committed to supporting others.

Developing the
Coach Mindset

"The moment I discovered coaching was through working with a coach. I became so inspired and came to realize that I was born for this. I did a lot of due diligence to find a program that was a match. As I continued searching, I was continually drawn to Thriving Coach Academy. I knew intuitively that this was right for me. Since enrolling, my financial success has blown my mind. Within three months, I had several clients hire me. I'm astounded by what I've accomplished in such a short time. Even before finishing the program, I had a month where I earned over $10,000 from coaching.

I see my business expanding in ways that will be beneficial not only to myself, but to others. For me, it's not only about the money. Becoming an effective coach, understanding the artistry of it, being part of a caring and supportive community—those things matter just as much. I have never felt so believed in as I have through TCA. I can't wait to wake up every morning to get started. If anybody is thinking that they're too old to learn something new, I started my business at 55 years old. I can't imagine retiring from it. We never know when our time is going to be up, so we might as well go in and do what we love."

– ALLISON C.

CHAPTER 8

The Coaching Arc

When it comes to being a successful coach, many people mistakenly believe they should focus on what happens during the coaching session itself. What they tend to overlook is that the most important groundwork takes place *before* the session even begins. The energy, awareness, and attitude you bring into a session can significantly influence the outcome. Coaching is not just about asking the right questions; it's about preparing your mind, heart, and environment to foster a space for true transformation.

One of the biggest challenges coaches face is feeling like their sessions are disorganized and scattered. They might struggle with knowing exactly what to focus on or feel like they're rushing through important parts. Sometimes, they may even find themselves finishing early and scrambling to fill the remaining time, unsure of what to say or ask next.

To address this issue, I developed a concept called the *Coaching Arc*. Once you grasp this framework, you'll never feel like your sessions are off track again. The Coaching Arc breaks down a session into three distinct parts: the beginning, the middle, and the end. Understanding this structure allows you to zoom out and see the big picture, helping you to focus on what's essential in each segment. By using this approach, you ensure each session feels purposeful, complete, and impactful.

The Coaching Arc

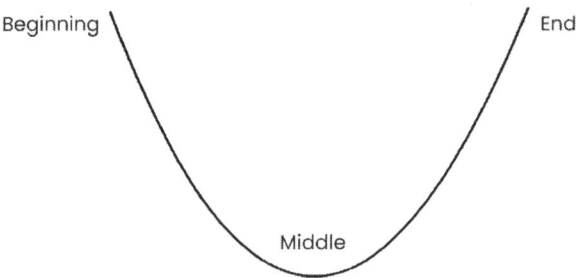

Let's dive into each part of the Coaching Arc and explore what you should focus on in each phase.

1. The Beginning: Setting the Stage for Success

Establishing Rapport

The first step in any successful coaching session is building rapport. Your clients need to feel comfortable, safe, and open to share their thoughts and feelings with you. Rapport is the foundation upon which trust is built. Without it, your clients might hold back, limiting the depth and helpfulness of the session.

Start by greeting your client warmly and engaging in light, casual conversation to break the ice. Make sure you're fully present and listen attentively, using non-verbal cues like eye contact, nodding, and mirroring their body language. This creates an environment where your client feels seen, heard, and valued, setting the tone for a productive session.

Clarifying the Agenda

After establishing rapport, it's time to clarify the session's agenda. This is where you help the client define the focus of the session. Without a clear agenda, the session can quickly become aimless, leading both you and the client to feel scattered. To help establish the agenda, you can ask questions like, "What would you like to achieve in today's session?" or, "How can I support you best today?"

Having a clear agenda ensures both you and your client are on the same page, aligning your efforts toward a specific outcome. It also provides structure, making it easier to stay focused on the most pressing issues. The agenda acts as a guide, preventing you from getting sidetracked and ensuring the session remains purposeful.

Identifying the Big Domino

Imagine a line of dominoes. When you knock over the first big one, all the others fall in a rhythmic sequence. This is what we refer to as the *Big Domino* in coaching. It represents the most significant issue or challenge that, when addressed, causes other, smaller issues to resolve themselves. Instead of tackling every problem your client presents, focus on identifying the Big Domino.

You can do this by asking, "Out of everything you've mentioned, which one feels like the heaviest or most urgent for you right now?" Once you've identified this core issue, you'll be ready to move into the middle of the session, where the real transformation begins.

2. The Middle: Guiding the Client Toward Breakthroughs

Exploring the Client's Rulebook

Every client operates according to an internal set of rules, beliefs, and assumptions—what we call their personal *Rulebook*. This rulebook shapes how they see the world, make decisions, and even how they respond to challenges. A key part of the coaching process is exploring the client's Rulebook and helping them recognize any limiting beliefs or outdated assumptions that are holding them back.

In Chapter 12: The Rulebook Coaching Method™, you will learn how to identify and transform their Old Rules, ultimately supporting their growth and success.

Asking Questions for Self-Discovery

The middle of the session is where the magic happens. This is where you guide your client through self-discovery by asking empowering and open-ended questions. Your role is not to provide answers, but to help your client uncover their own insights and solutions. The right questions will encourage your client to reflect deeply and tap into their inner wisdom.

In Chapter 15: The Four Flavors of Curiosity, you will learn how to ask questions that will provoke thought and inspire breakthrough moments.

3. The End: Bringing It All Together

Summarizing Key Takeaways

As the session nears its end, it's important to summarize the key takeaways from your time together. This reinforces the insights gained and helps the client see how far they've come within the session. Reflect on the progress made and highlight any significant moments of discovery. This not only gives the client a sense of accomplishment but also reinforces the value of the coaching process.

Action Planning

No coaching session is complete without a plan of action. Help your client translate their newfound insights into concrete steps they can take after the session. Ask questions like, "What's the first step you'll take to apply this new awareness?" or, "How will you hold yourself accountable for this change?" Creating a clear action plan ensures that the momentum continues beyond the session.

Establish Accountability

It's not enough for a client to leave with great insights or a beautiful goal; they need to have a plan in place to take action on what they've discovered. Without accountability, even the best of intentions can fall flat. This is where you ask your client to commit to specific actions and set clear deadlines.

For example, if a client has decided they want to go to the gym more regularly, ask, "When will you go to the gym? What days work best for you?" Probe further by asking, "Is anything likely to get in the way of this plan? How can you overcome that obstacle?" By establishing accountability, you ensure that your clients not only leave the session inspired but also equipped to follow through on their commitments.

In Chapter 20: Finishing Sessions Strong, you will learn how to tie a bow on your sessions in a way that leaves clients inspired and ready for action.

Mastering the Art of Coaching

You might wonder about the ideal length for a coaching session. Is twenty minutes enough? Should it be a full hour? The truth is, the length of the session doesn't matter nearly as much as how well you honor the Coaching Arc. Whether the session is short or long, the most critical thing is to create a natural flow through the beginning, middle, and end. This framework ensures that your clients will leave with a sense of completion, regardless of how much time was spent.

Understanding the Coaching Arc is key to mastering the art of coaching. By structuring your sessions with a clear beginning, middle, and end, you create a powerful and effective framework that guides both you and your clients toward success. This approach not only improves the quality of your sessions but also enhances the overall client experience.

When you honor the Coaching Arc, your clients will leave each session with a deeper sense of accomplishment and clarity, while you'll feel more confident in your ability to guide them through meaningful transformations. Remember, the success of a coaching session isn't just about what happens in the moment—it's about the preparation, the flow, and the intentionality you bring to each part of the process.

CHAPTER 9

Seeing Your Clients As Heroes

Years ago, I mentored a coach who shared a story about one of her clients who seemed stuck in her struggles. The coach was perplexed by the difficulties she was experiencing. I asked her a simple question: "Do you believe in this client?"

After a long pause, she hesitated and replied, "I believe in her...half of the time."

And that was the problem. It wasn't the client's struggle that was the issue; it was the coach's reluctance to fully believe in her client's potential. When coaches don't wholeheartedly believe in their clients, they fall into the trap of seeing them as people who need to be rescued, healed, or saved. Instead of empowering their clients, they end up coddling them, unintentionally reinforcing the idea that the client is incapable of solving their own problems.

This story illustrates a fundamental principle in coaching: the importance of seeing your clients not as victims, but as heroes on an epic adventure. When a coach sees their client as a hero, they create a relationship built on strength, respect, and unwavering belief in the client's ability to overcome challenges.

It's easy for a coach to slip into the role of a "savior," feeling they need to remove obstacles or provide all the answers. But real growth happens when clients are given the space and encouragement to uncover their own resilience.

Seeing your clients as heroes means recognizing their strengths even when they can't, believing in their potential when they doubt it, and holding them accountable instead of protecting them from discomfort. A hero doesn't need rescuing; they need a guide to help them find their own courage.

Compassion vs. Coddling

If you see clients as victims, you might feel compelled to coddle them or take on the responsibility of solving their problems. You might feel bad when they share their challenges, believing it's your job to alleviate their pain or suffering. However, your clients are not broken, and therefore they do not need to be fixed. They are whole and complete, with all the answers within themselves, waiting to be uncovered.

Coddling manifests as the desire to get your clients out of pain or to end their suffering. If you catch yourself thinking, "I feel bad for my clients," you risk falling into the trap of coddling. This approach undermines their abilities to grow and discover their own solutions. Instead, you must encourage them to believe in their own strength and resilience.

Some might raise the concern, "What about being compassionate?" Compassion is indeed essential for helpful coaching, but it can easily be confused with coddling. Compassion means understanding and sympathizing with someone's struggles *without* diminishing their own strength. Coddling involves overprotecting a client from discomfort, stepping in to solve their problems, or taking on their struggles as if it's the coach's responsibility. When a coach coddles, they unintentionally undermine the client's potential by removing the very challenges that could lead to growth.

Avoiding coddling and choosing compassion doesn't mean you don't care about their problem or are dismissing it. Instead, it means you're acknowledging the challenge while seeing them as a hero who can overcome it.

> *True compassion involves being a loving witness to someone's challenges and inspiring them to show up for themselves. It's about recognizing their potential and reminding them of how powerful they are.*

For instance, consider a coach working with a client who lost their job. If the coach were coddling, they might say,

"This is so unfair to you. You've been dealt such a bad hand, and it's no wonder you're feeling hopeless." While this may sound caring, it subtly implies that the client isn't capable of handling the challenge, and it can encourage avoidance rather than growth.

Instead of rushing in to comfort them or offer quick solutions, the coach might say, "I can see how hard this is for you. Losing a job can bring up many emotions and fears. Let's explore what this experience means to you and what strengths you can bring moving forward."

This approach validates the client's experience while encouraging them to take ownership of their next steps. The coach acknowledges the difficulty of the situation without taking on the burden to fix it—rather, they are helping the client find their own resilience.

The distinction is crucial: compassion involves support and encouragement, while coddling can lead to dependency and stunted growth. When we coddle our clients, we may inadvertently suggest the client is incapable of overcoming their struggles, which diminishes their confidence and reinforces a victim mentality.

How a Coach Responds

Understanding how you should respond to clients is vital in fostering a transformative coaching relationship. The language you use can either uplift or undermine their journey.

When coaches view their clients as victims, their responses might include phrases like:

- Maybe you should take it easy and not push yourself too hard.

- I don't know how you'll manage to get through this.
- Let me handle and fix this for you.
- I understand if you want to give up.
- I feel bad for you.

These responses can unintentionally make the client feel helpless and limit their potential. In contrast, when coaches see their clients as heroes, their responses shift to more empowering language, such as:

- I know you have the ability to overcome this.
- You have the skills and resilience to navigate this situation.
- How can we use your strengths to address this challenge?
- Let's explore the possibilities and find a way forward.
- Remember how capable you are. You've got this.

By consciously choosing language that reinforces your belief in their abilities, you help clients tap into their own strength and resilience, allowing them to rise to challenges and achieve their goals.

The Transformation Process

As coaches, we often see our clients during significant transformation phases. These might include career changes, health and fitness goals, or relationship challenges. Think of your clients as caterpillars in a cocoon, undergoing their metamorphosis. Just as a butterfly must struggle to emerge from its chrysalis, your clients must confront their challenges and discomfort to evolve into their best selves. If we intervene too soon, we risk harming their growth.

In this light, remember: it's not your job to keep your client comfortable. Growth requires discomfort. Just like muscles need to tear in the gym to grow stronger, clients often need to face their fears and stretch beyond their comfort zones in order to grow. Your role is to hold space for this discomfort and support them through it, trusting that it's essential to their transformation.

It's essential to adopt a mindset that acknowledges their heroism. Here are some thoughts to embrace about your clients:

- I see my client as the hero of their journey, capable of overcoming challenges and achieving their goals.
- I trust the process and my client's ability to find their answers.
- I won't rush to provide solutions; I will allow for self-discovery.
- I'm here to empower my client, not rescue them.

When you reframe your perspective and see every coaching session as a turning point in your client's epic adventure, you cultivate an empowering environment. Instead of viewing them as hitting a wall, see them as navigating a speed bump on their journey. You become a witness to their heroism, awakening the hero within them.

The Gift of Belief

In the world of coaching, believing in your clients is one of the most profound gifts you can offer. Imagine the impact on someone who, for perhaps the first time, encounters a person who believes unwaveringly in their potential and vision. This belief is not just a motivational tool; it's a transformative force.

How much do you believe in the human capacity to change, even in unfavorable circumstances? There are always going to be things out of our control—like the economy, time, or money. These external factors should not define your clients' lives. Heroes realize they can create their dream lives even in unfavorable circumstances. It's not our circumstances that define us; it's our decisions. As Randy Pausch famously said, "We can't change the cards that we are dealt, but we can change how we play the hand."

By seeing your clients as heroes rather than victims, you empower them to navigate their challenges and emerge stronger. Compassionate coaching involves recognizing their struggles while encouraging their inherent strength and resilience. With the right mindset and language, you can foster an environment where clients feel supported in their journeys toward transformation.

CHAPTER 10

Embracing Infinite Possibilities

magine an artist standing before a blank canvas, filled with endless possibilities. There are no boundaries, no rules—just a space where creativity can flow freely.

Now, think of coaching in the same way. Each client that sits in front of you is like a blank canvas. They have their own experiences, desires, and goals, but nothing is predetermined about where they can go. When you, as the coach, show up with an open mind—without assumptions, biases, or preconceived ideas—you create the space for your client to explore their own potential. This is what I call honoring the Blank Canvas.

Honoring the Blank Canvas means approaching each session with the understanding that your client holds infinite possibilities within them. They are capable of creating something entirely new and unique in their lives. But—and this is key—it's *their* canvas, not yours. Your job is to facilitate their exploration, not dictate what should be painted on it.

Let's dive deeper into why honoring the Blank Canvas is crucial in coaching and how showing up with this mindset can lead to transformative breakthroughs.

The Power of the Blank Canvas

When an artist starts with a blank canvas, they're not confined to a single outcome. They can add vibrant colors, explore abstract forms, or create something realistic. Similarly, when you show up to a coaching session with a Blank Canvas, you open the door for your client to discover what truly resonates with them. Infinite possibilities are on the table, and they get to decide what they want to create.

The problem arises when coaches unintentionally bring their biases into the session. It's easy to fall into the trap of thinking, "I know exactly what this client needs!" Maybe you've seen someone go through a similar challenge or have your own experience to draw from. While your intentions might be good, overlaying your perspective on the client limits their exploration.

When a client comes to you struggling with their career, they might state they feel unmotivated and want to explore new possibilities. A coach who doesn't understand the Blank Canvas might jump in with advice like, "You need to take on a leadership role. Leadership positions are where the real satisfaction is. Trust me, I've seen it before!"

Sure, the coach feels like they've provided value. But here's the issue: the assumption is based on the coach's personal bias. The client's dissatisfaction is being funneled toward a solution that may not even align with their values, skills, or long-term desires. What if the client isn't interested in management? What if leadership isn't where they'll find fulfillment? Perhaps they would feel more satisfied in a role that allows for hands-on, project-based work rather than overseeing others.

By pushing your own agenda, even with the best intentions at heart, you're limiting the client's potential to find the solution that best fits them. You're painting on their canvas instead of handing them the brush.

A more helpful response would be to ask open-ended questions that encourage the client to explore their own motivations and desires. For example, you could ask, "What kind of work have you done in the past that you found most energizing?" or "What aspects of your current role do you enjoy most, even on challenging days?"

These questions allow the client to reflect on their experiences, guiding them to uncover what truly brings them fulfillment. By keeping the session client-centered, you empower them to identify a path that resonates deeply with who they are.

Don't Paint Over Their Canvas

Let's look at another scenario. A client is faced with a huge life decision: they've been offered a high-paying job in a different city, but they're unsure whether to take it or stay where they're comfortable. A coach not embracing the Blank Canvas might say, "You've got to take the job! You'll make more money, expand your network, and gain new experiences. It's a no-brainer!"

While this advice might seem sound on the surface, it's driven by the coach's own biases—biases about what success looks like and what opportunities matter most. But what if the client values stability over adventure? What if they're more connected to their current community than the financial gain from the new job?

Instead, you can support them by asking questions that bring clarity to their priorities. For instance, you could ask, "What does each option represent for you in terms of your personal values?" or, "What would your ideal outcome look like in this situation?" By encouraging the client to explore these deeper reflections, you help them connect with what truly matters to them, free of outside influence.

This is the core of working with a Blank Canvas—it's not about what *you* think is best for the client; it's about what *they* feel is right. Your role is to create a space for them to explore their values, desires, and goals without interference. You're not there to direct them but to guide them through their own self-discovery.

Shifting Your Mindset as a Coach

To honor the Blank Canvas, you need to adopt a specific mindset when you approach each coaching session. Here are key beliefs to anchor yourself in:

1. **Curiosity over Certainty**. Be genuinely curious about where your client is coming from. They are the expert on their life, not you.

   Reflective Question: am I truly hearing my client, or am I waiting to insert my advice?

2. **Facilitating, Not Directing**. You're there to facilitate your client's growth, not impose your own ideas. This requires letting go of attachment to a particular outcome.

   Reflective Question: how can I help my client explore without steering the conversation in a particular direction?

3. **Their Success, Their Terms**. Your client defines success, not you. What might look like a missed opportunity in your eyes could be exactly what they need.

   Reflective Question: how can I honor what my client defines as success, even if it's different from what I'd choose?

4. **Stay Open to Surprises**. Allow yourself to be surprised. Often, clients will discover things about themselves that you might not have anticipated—and that's a good thing!

   Reflective Question: am I open to unexpected breakthroughs, or am I clinging to a particular outcome?

5. **Respect Their Autonomy**. Your client has the right to make their own decisions—even if they don't align with your suggestions. Respecting their autonomy builds trust and fosters empowerment.

   Reflective Question: am I empowering my client to take ownership of their decisions?

This approach empowers your client to take ownership of their journey, allowing them to craft solutions that are uniquely their own.

Having a Blank Canvas is about letting go of your need to direct the process. It's about trusting your client to find their own way forward. When you stop trying to paint on their canvas and instead hand them the brush, you open the door to deeper, more meaningful growth. In short, it's not about what you think should be created—it's about what your client is inspired to create.

So next time you're in a session, ask yourself: am I allowing the client to have a Blank Canvas? Or am I already halfway through painting on it?

CHAPTER 11

Why Coaching Isn't Always Easy

'll never forget the moment that changed how I think about mastery. Last month, I was at tennis camp, eagerly awaiting instruction from the head coach. It was a hot afternoon, and we were all standing by the court, watching some of the camp's best players warm up. The head coach asked us, "If you had to describe how a professional serves the ball in one word, what would it be?"

We tossed out answers like "powerful," "fast," and "precise," but he shook his head.

When the volley of answers stopped, he told us, "Effortless."

The word hit me like a brick. That's exactly how coaching feels to me now—effortless. But it wasn't always that way. When I started, coaching was anything but effortless. I struggled daily. I overthought every interaction, every question, every response. Anxiety would rise every time I faced a new client, wondering if I would be able to deliver the breakthroughs they expected. But, with time, I learned struggling is simply part of the process.

Coaching isn't always easy. It's not supposed to be, especially in the beginning. Much like learning any new skill, coaching requires time, practice, and patience before it becomes second nature. What feels difficult and clunky today will one day feel smooth and natural. The secret lies in understanding the learning process and embracing it, rather than resisting it.

The Four Stages of Learning

To understand why coaching feels hard in the beginning, it's helpful to know the four stages of learning. These stages explain why we struggle at first and, eventually, why we don't.

1. **Unconscious Incompetence**. In this stage, you don't know what you don't know. You may have heard about coaching or watched others do it and thought, "How hard can it be?" But when you start, you quickly realize there's a

lot you haven't yet learned. The gap between where you are and where you want to be feels overwhelming. This stage can be deceiving because the initial excitement of becoming a coach often masks how far you have yet to go. You're still full of hope, but reality hits hard when you face your first difficult client session.

2. **Conscious Incompetence**. This is the "wake-up call" stage, where frustration sets in. You're aware of your limitations, and suddenly the gap between what you know and what you need to know seems enormous. You become acutely aware of what you're not good at. Maybe you're struggling to ask powerful questions or feeling uncertain about how to guide a session. It's easy to feel discouraged because you know what you should be doing but you aren't doing it well yet. Many people quit at this stage because it feels uncomfortable. But this uncomfortable place is where the most growth happens. The ability to tolerate the frustration of this stage is what separates those who eventually master coaching from those who give up.

3. **Conscious Competence**. Here's where things start to get better. You're improving, but you're still very aware of what you're doing. You can coach effectively, but it requires effort and focus. Every question, every response is deliberate, and while you're no longer struggling as much, it doesn't yet feel natural. You may start seeing positive outcomes with clients, but you still have to be on your toes. This stage demands mental energy as you're consciously making choices in your sessions, double-checking your work, and actively seeking ways to improve.

4. **Unconscious Competence**. This is where mastery lives. At this stage, coaching flows. You've integrated all the skills and techniques so deeply that they're automatic. You're not thinking about what to say next; it just comes to you. You've internalized the process, and it feels effortless—like that professional tennis player serving the ball. This is the place where coaching feels like second nature, and this is the stage where many coaches begin to see the true impact of their work. They're no longer concerned with "getting it right," and instead, they're focused on being fully present with their clients. Coaching becomes intuitive, and this is where the magic happens.

On the first day of training, I always tell my coaching students: whenever you catch yourself saying "I'm struggling," replace it with "I'm learning." When you think you're struggling, it can feel like there's a real problem—but there isn't. You're simply in the growth phase. Mastery takes time, so give yourself grace and trust the process.

When you embrace each stage of learning, you take the pressure off yourself. You're no longer expecting perfection from the start. One day, you'll wake up and realize the fear and self-doubt you have as a coach are gone. Coaching will flow effortlessly, just like that tennis pro's serve.

Until then, give yourself permission to be a learner. Allow yourself to be imperfect. Remember, the challenges you face now won't last forever—and with each step, you're becoming the coach you're meant to be.

Which Stage Are You In?

Below is a quick self-assessment to help you identify where you might be in your coaching journey. Read through each stage and see which set of statements resonates most with your experience right now.

Stage 1: Unconscious Incompetence

- "I'm excited about coaching but unsure what it really takes."
- "I don't know what I don't know yet."
- "I'm discovering how much more there is to learn."

Stage 2: Conscious Incompetence

- "I'm aware of my limitations, and it's frustrating."
- "I second-guess most coaching conversations I have."
- "I sometimes doubt if I'm cut out for this."

Stage 3: Conscious Competence

- "I'm more confident now, but I can still spot areas for improvement."
- "Coaching is getting easier, yet I still have to be deliberate."
- "I'm seeing progress, but it's not second nature yet."

Stage 4: Unconscious Competence

- "Coaching flows naturally and intuitively."
- "I trust myself to ask the right questions at the right time."
- "Sessions feel effortless—I'm fully present in the moment."

If you're not at Stage 4 yet, ask yourself:

- Where can I find the support I need to progress?

- Who could mentor me and share their experiences?
- How can I connect with a community of like-minded coaches?

Remember, you don't have to do this alone. Embrace each stage of learning and lean on the right people to guide you. One day, you'll look up and realize that coaching has become truly *effortless*.

CHAPTER 12

The Rulebook Coaching Method™

F or most of my life, I was shy, insecure, and lacked confidence. Fear held me back from sharing my voice and stepping into the spotlight. But then, a pivotal moment happened—one that would forever alter the course of my life.

After graduating from college, I made the bold decision to teach English in China. Something about the idea of moving halfway across the world called to me. It's hard to explain, but I felt drawn to embrace the adventure, to step into the unknown. I booked my ticket and prepared for the sixteen-hour flight from New York to Shanghai. I was terrified, yes, but I was excited too.

The moment I stepped off the plane, I was in a world that felt entirely new. The air was thick with the smell of spices and humidity, and rapid-fire conversations in Mandarin buzzed around me. Everything around me—the people, the language, the pace of life—was unfamiliar. It was overwhelming, yet freeing.

Before this, I had a set idea about who I was as a person. But in this new environment, where no one knew me, I realized something profound: I could be whoever I wanted to be. I no longer had to be the quiet, insecure person who faded into the background. I could choose to be someone who spoke up, someone who believed they had something important to say.

It was as if I had a Rulebook in my back pocket, one I hadn't even realized existed. This Rulebook was filled with all the assumptions, beliefs, and expectations I had about myself and the world around me. And for the first time, I understood that I could rewrite those Rules.

You don't need to travel across the world to experience this kind of transformation. The truth is, you can do this work right where you are. The rules that shape your life are the product of your past experiences, your upbringing, your environment, and your beliefs. But here's the crucial part: you have the power to rewrite those Rules.

Understanding the Rules that Shape Us

Rules are the implicit or explicit guidelines that govern our lives. These Rules encompass our beliefs, expectations, and assumptions about ourselves, others, and the world. We all carry these rules, often without even realizing it. And while some of them serve us well, many of them hold us back from reaching our full potential.

Rules are shaped by various factors, including:

1. **Upbringing**. Many values and norms are instilled in us during childhood by parents, caregivers, and authority figures.
2. **Social Environment**. Media, societal norms, and peers shape our rules about success, beauty, relationships, and more.
3. **Education**. Teachers and mentors impart beliefs about achievement, intelligence, and personal worth.
4. **Family Roles**. The dynamics within our families can influence our beliefs about identity and responsibility.
5. **Religion and Spirituality**. Religious teachings often shape our moral values, ethical standards, and beliefs about purpose.

The key to transforming your life is in identifying these rules, challenging them, and rewriting the ones that no longer serve you.

When I began my coaching practice, I noticed a fascinating pattern. My clients, like me, were bound by their own unspoken rules. These rules dictated who they should be, what they could achieve, and how they should interact with the world. Most importantly, these rules were holding them back from experiencing breakthroughs.

Determined to help my clients break free from their limiting beliefs, I developed a three-step process called The Rulebook Coaching Method™. This method involves helping clients:

1. **Identify** the Rules that are shaping their lives.
2. **Challenge** those Rules by questioning their validity.
3. **Rewrite** the Rules to align with the person they want to become.

After years of refining this process, The Rulebook Coaching Method™ has become the most efficient tool for facilitating breakthroughs. By focusing on a client's core beliefs, this method creates profound and lasting change.

The Science Behind Rulebook Coaching

The Rulebook Coaching Method™ is not just a theoretical approach; it is grounded in scientifically proven concepts, particularly neuroplasticity and positive psychology, with some overlap with cognitive behavioral therapy (CBT) principles. Together, these concepts explain why the method works so effectively.

Neuroplasticity

Neuroplasticity refers to the brain's ability to reorganize itself by forming new neural connections. When clients identify a limiting belief (or Rule), they are recognizing a neural pathway that has been reinforced over time through repeated thoughts and behaviors. The more a belief is repeated, the stronger that neural pathway becomes.

By using The Rulebook Coaching Method™ to challenge and rewrite these beliefs, clients begin to form new neural connections. With time and practice, these new connections become stronger, and the old, limiting beliefs fade away. This process of rewiring the brain allows clients to adopt more empowering rules that align with their goals and aspirations.

Positive Psychology

Positive psychology focuses on cultivating strengths, fostering resilience, and enhancing well-being. Rather than concentrating on what's wrong, positive psychology emphasizes what is working and how individuals can build on that to thrive.

The Rulebook Coaching Method™ aligns perfectly with this approach. By helping clients rewrite the things that are limiting them, you are enabling them to focus on their strengths and capabilities. This method promotes a mindset of growth, optimism, and possibility, which allows clients to shift their focus away from fear or doubt and toward what they can achieve. When clients rewrite their Rules in this empowering way, they are tapping into the principles of positive psychology, boosting their sense of well-being, and unlocking their potential for success.

Cognitive Behavioral Therapy

Though The Rulebook Coaching Method™ is distinct from therapy, there is some overlap with the principles of cognitive behavioral therapy (CBT). CBT is a well-established psychological approach that helps people identify and challenge distorted thinking patterns in order to develop healthier, more productive thoughts and behaviors.

Similarly, in The Rulebook Coaching Method™, clients are encouraged to challenge their existing Rules—beliefs that are often rooted in past experiences but may no longer serve them. This overlap with CBT involves helping clients question the validity of these limiting beliefs and replace them with new, empowering thoughts. However, unlike CBT, which is designed to treat mental health issues, The Rulebook Coaching Method™ is focused on personal growth, transformation, and thriving, making it perfectly suited for a coaching environment.

Why Rulebook Coaching Works

What truly sets The Rulebook Coaching Method™ apart is its ability to address the root causes of a client's challenges, rather than just focusing on surface-level symptoms. Traditional coaching methods often help clients set goals or develop strategies to overcome obstacles, but they don't always address the underlying beliefs that shape a person's actions.

A rule is a single-sentence belief that governs how we see ourselves and the world. While some rules may seem factual, it's important to remember that they are all subjective. For instance, a common rule might be, "Success requires hard work." This isn't an absolute truth—it's simply a belief that shapes a person's experience.

Rules can either work for us or they can work against us. The rules you've been playing by up until now have gotten you to where you are in life—in your career, your relationships, your health, etc. But leveling up requires examining those Rules to see which ones need to be rewritten.

The beauty of The Rulebook Coaching Method™ is that it allows clients to gain awareness of the Rules they are living by and empowers them to create new, more empowering ones. As a coach, this method enables you to dive deep into the core of your client's belief system, creating rapid and transformative breakthroughs.

> ### The more you master The Rulebook Coaching Method™, the more impactful your coaching practice will become.

Your clients will begin to present their Rulebook to you during sessions without even realizing it. They will reveal the Rules that govern their lives, and if you don't know how to recognize them, you'll miss the opportunity to create true transformation.

When you apply Rulebook Coaching, you coach the person, not just the problem. This method allows you to see beyond the surface and address the deeper beliefs shaping your client's reality.

As long as you can effectively use The Rulebook Coaching Method™, you will stand out as a transformational coach. You'll be able to guide your clients through their most profound breakthroughs, and in doing so, you'll build a practice that is both successful and fulfilling.

In the next chapter, I will reveal the three simple steps to mastering The Rulebook Coaching Method™. Once you learn how to recognize and rewrite your clients' Rules, you will have a powerful tool at your disposal—one that will set you apart and ensure that your clients achieve lasting, life-changing results.

CHAPTER 13

The Three Steps to Reinvention

As we've discussed in the previous chapter, one of the most powerful aspects of coaching is the ability to help individuals recognize and transform the invisible rules that govern their lives. These internalized beliefs, often operating beneath the surface, can shape decisions, limit potential, and keep people stuck in patterns that no longer serve them. The Rulebook Coaching Method™ is designed to empower clients to identify these limiting beliefs, challenge them, and ultimately replace them with empowering, growth-oriented rules.

Now, I'm going to guide you through the three essential steps of The Rulebook Coaching Method™: Identify the Old Rule, Challenge the Old Rule, and Create the New Rule. After this chapter, you will be able to apply these steps with your clients to create lasting change.

Step 1: Identify the Old Rule

This initial step involves pinpointing the existing rule or belief that is holding the client back. It's about bringing awareness to the subconscious patterns and thought processes that have been governing their actions and decisions.

Identifying the Old Rule is essential because it allows the individual to clearly see the constraints they've been operating under, often without even realizing it. This awareness is the first step toward making change, as it provides a starting point for challenging and, eventually, dismantling these limiting beliefs.

Here's what this sounds like in a session:

"May I make an observation? I am hearing that you may have a rule/expectation/assumption/idea that [insert Old Rule here]. Do you hear that as well?"

For example: *"I'm hearing that you may have a rule or expectation around always putting others' needs before your own. Would you agree?"*

Step 2: Challenge the Old Rule

Once the Old Rule has been identified, the next step is questioning its validity and challenging its hold over the individual's mindset. This is where you "poke holes" at the Old Rule and invite your client to question the underlying assumptions and beliefs that have shaped their thinking. By challenging the Old Rule, your client begins to loosen their grip and open themselves to the possibility of new perspectives and beliefs.

Here are some key questions to ask during this phase:

- How do you feel when you think (Old Rule)?
- What is it costing you to think (Old Rule)?
- How true is it that (Old Rule)?
- What evidence do you have that (Old Rule) might not be true?
- What are some exceptions or instances where this rule doesn't apply?
- Who would you be without the idea that (Old Rule)?

Your goal is to ask as many questions as necessary until the client indicates some form of uncertainty about their Old Rule. Here are some common phrases clients may use to indicate doubt about the Old Rule:

- I've always believed that, but now I'm starting to wonder...
- I've never really questioned it before, but now I'm thinking...
- I used to think that way, but lately, I've been reconsidering...
- I suppose the Old Rule I had may not be entirely true...

These statements signal that the client is opening up to new possibilities and is ready to move forward with the transformation process.

This second step is one many coaches forget. Jumping too quickly into creating a New Rule before the client has fully released the old one can feel forced. Make sure there's enough cognitive space for the new belief to take root.

Step 3: Create the New Rule

With the Old Rule dismantled, the final step is replacing it with a New Rule. This step is about consciously choosing a mindset that aligns with who the person wants to become. The New Rule will serve as a guiding principle that will inspire the client to take bold action and pursue their dreams with confidence.

Here are some questions to guide the creation of the New Rule:

- What would you like to believe instead?
- What else could be true instead of the Old Rule you've been operating under?
- What empowering belief would you like to replace the Old Rule with?

You may wonder, *"What if a client says their Old Rule is true? What if they double-down on their limiting belief?"* The approach is simple: just because something is true doesn't mean you have to focus on it. If something negative or limiting is true, it doesn't mean you must devote all your attention to it. You can still control where to place your focus, shifting toward solutions and opportunities instead of limitations.

Here are three scenarios so you can see what The Rulebook Coaching Method™ looks like when it is brought to life. All of these scenarios come from real coaching sessions.

Scenario 1:
"My past defines me. I can't do something because I haven't done it before."

Step 1: Identify the Old Rule

Client: I've been struggling with taking on new projects at work. I haven't done anything like this before, so I don't think I can do it.

Coach: May I make an observation? I am hearing that you may have a rule that your past defines you and you can't do something because you haven't done it before. Do you hear that as well?

Client: Yes, I think that's true. I've always felt limited by what I've done in the past.

Step 2: Challenge the Old Rule

Coach: How do you feel when you think that your past defines you?

Client: I feel stuck and hopeless, like there's no way for me to change or improve.

Coach: How true is it that your past defines you?

Client: I guess it's not entirely true. People can change, and I've seen others do things they've never done before.

Coach: Who would you be without the idea that your past defines you?

Client: I would be more confident and open to new opportunities.

Step 3: Create the New Rule

Coach: Excellent! And what New Rule would you like to replace the Old Rule with?

Client: I am capable of achieving new things, regardless of my past experiences.

Coach: That's a powerful new belief. How does it feel to think that you're capable of achieving new things?

Client: It feels liberating. I feel like I can move forward without being stuck in the past.

In this scenario, the client begins with a limiting belief that their past defines their ability to take on new challenges. Through The Rulebook Coaching Method™, they identify this Old Rule, challenge it by exploring its impact, and ultimately replace it with an empowering New Rule that opens them up to new possibilities and confidence in their future potential.

Scenario 2:
"I can't start something until I feel ready."

Step 1: Identify the Old Rule

Client: I have this great business idea, but I keep postponing it because I don't feel ready. I think I need more time to prepare.

Coach: May I share something? I am hearing that you may have a rule that you can't start or do something until you feel ready. Do you notice that as well?

Client: Yes, that's exactly how I feel. I always wait until I feel completely prepared.

Step 2: Challenge the Old Rule

Coach: When you think you can't start until you feel ready, how does that hold you back?

Client: It's preventing me from taking action and achieving my goals.

Coach: So, how true is it *really* that you can't start something until you feel ready?

Client: It's not entirely true. I've done things in the past before feeling ready, and they turned out fine.

Coach: What evidence do you have that this rule might not be true?

Client: I've heard many successful people say they started without feeling fully prepared.

Step 3: Create the New Rule

Coach: What New Rule would you like to replace the Old Rule with?

Client: I can start something *before* I feel ready. I can allow myself to grow and learn as I go.

Coach: How might starting before you feel ready open up new opportunities for you?

Client: I think I'd make progress faster. Waiting for the perfect moment has only delayed everything.

In this scenario, the client holds the belief that they can't start their business until they feel fully prepared, which has led to delays and inaction. Through The Rulebook Coaching

Method™, the client identifies and challenges this Old Rule, realizing that progress can be made even without perfect readiness. By adopting a New Rule that allows for growth and learning along the way, the client is empowered to take immediate steps toward their goals.

Scenario 3:
"Putting yourself first is selfish or wrong."

Step 1: Identify the Old Rule

Client: I feel guilty when I take time for myself. I worry that putting my needs first is selfish.

Coach: May I point something out? I am hearing that you may have a rule that putting yourself first is selfish or wrong. Do you hear that as well?

Client: Yes, I always feel guilty when I put my needs before others.

Step 2: Challenge the Old Rule

Coach: What is it costing you to think that putting yourself first is selfish or wrong?

Client: It's making me neglect my own needs and well-being.

Coach: How true then that putting yourself first is selfish or wrong?

Client: I suppose it's not entirely true. Taking care of myself can actually help me take better care of others.

Coach: What would change for you if you released the idea that putting yourself first is selfish or wrong?

Client: I would be more balanced and better able to meet my own needs as well as others'.

Step 3: Create the New Rule

Coach: What empowering belief would you like to replace the Old Rule with?

Client: Taking care of myself helps me take better care of others.

Coach: That's a powerful shift. How do you imagine your relationships will change when you start prioritizing your own needs?

Client: I think I'll have more energy and patience to give to others because I'll be taking care of myself first.

In this scenario, the client initially believes that putting themselves first is selfish, leading to guilt and neglect of their own needs. Through The Rulebook Coaching Method™, the client challenges and shifts this Old Rule, realizing that self-care enhances their ability to support others. By adopting a New Rule that prioritizes their well-being, they feel empowered to make healthier, guilt-free choices in their daily life.

As you review these scenarios, you may have some reservations. Let's discuss a few common ones.

"It seems too structured, and I like a more flexible approach to coaching."

That's fine! While The Rulebook Coaching Method™ offers a structured framework, it's designed to be adaptable. The steps guide the client through a transformation process, but you still have the flexibility to tailor your questions, adapt the pacing, and explore what comes up organically in each session. The structure ensures you don't skip any of the important steps, but within that, there's plenty of room for creativity and flow.

"What if the client doesn't come up with a new empowering belief on their own?"

They probably won't do this right away. Creating the New Rule doesn't have to happen in a single session and it should not feel forced. Sometimes, clients need time to process and let go of the Old Rule before they can fully embrace a new one. If the client struggles, you can guide them by suggesting empowering alternatives and asking how those beliefs might feel, or brainstorming ways they can change their approach. Ultimately, the client is in charge of adopting the New Rule, but you are there to support them through thoughtful questions and encouragement.

"What if my client doesn't realize they have an Old Rule or resists challenging it?"

It's common for clients to resist recognizing their limiting beliefs initially, which is why The Rulebook Coaching Method™ starts with compassionate questioning and observation. When they resist, gentle exploration of how the belief affects them can open the door to deeper reflection. Over time, the client will likely begin to see the impact of their Old Rule on their life, allowing for more openness to change.

"What if my clients don't resonate with the idea of 'rules' or feel it's too rigid?"

The concept of "rules" can be adjusted to fit the client's language. If the word "rule" feels too rigid, you can refer to it as a belief, assumption, or mindset. The essence of the method is identifying limiting beliefs, challenging them, and creating new, empowering perspectives. The terminology used to address these points can be flexible to ensure it resonates with your clients, while still achieving the same transformative results.

Mastering The Rulebook Coaching Method™ is a game changer for both you and your clients. Once you become skilled in guiding clients through these three simple yet powerful steps—identifying their limiting beliefs, challenging them, and creating empowering New Rules—you'll be able to facilitate breakthroughs in just minutes.

Clients will be blown away by the speed and depth of their transformation, often experiencing shifts in mindset that they never thought possible. By mastering this method, you'll not only build trust and confidence in your coaching practice but also consistently deliver life-changing results that leave your clients inspired and ready to take bold action in their lives.

In the next section, you'll move from mindset to mastery, honing the core skills that make coaching truly transformative. You'll master the art of listening, learn the four flavors of curiosity and discover how to bring sessions to a powerful close. With these tools, you'll be able to take your coaching to a whole new level, guiding clients toward the achievement of profound and lasting transformation.

TOP 10 INSIGHTS

1. Your impact as a coach begins before the session, in the way you show up—through the awareness, energy, and attitude you bring.

2. At the beginning of a session, the goal is to identify the Big Domino, or the most pressing challenge your client wants to address.

3. In the middle of a session, the goal is to explore the client's internal Rulebook and uncover limiting beliefs holding them back.

4. At the end of a session, the goal is to define a clear action step and hold your client accountable for moving forward.

5. See your clients as heroes, not victims—you are not there to rescue, fix, heal, or save, but to help them uncover their own strength and resilience.

6. Release your bias and assumptions about what's best for your clients, and show up to sessions with a Blank Canvas, allowing your client to define their own path.

7. With the right mentorship and practice, coaching will become second nature—an effortless flow where you trust your instincts and guide clients with confidence.

8. Our lives are shaped by Rules that govern our beliefs, actions, and decisions—often without us realizing it.

9. The key to transformation lies in identifying and understanding the spoken and unspoken Rules that hold your client back.

10. The three steps of the Rulebook Coaching Method™ are: Identify the Old Rule, Challenge the Old Rule, and Create the New Rule.

Mastering the Art of Coaching

"I first discovered coaching when my management consulting firm offered an executive coach to support our team. When I left that firm, I hired her personally and have been excited about making it my career journey ever since. After my first weekend of training with Thriving Coach Academy, I enrolled two paid clients. Since then, my coaching has been more in demand than I expected. A big shift that had to take place in my mind in order to enroll paid clients was to start trusting myself to really pursue this path. Everywhere I go in my life, I'm meeting people I can help. I've now raised my rates to a point where I am making three times the hourly rate that I used to make when I worked in corporate strategy in tech.

As a twenty-five-year-old, I've realized my age has nothing to do with my ability to coach. My coaching ability is based on factors that are intrinsic to my ability to connect with other humans, listen powerfully, and ask empowering questions. The only thing I wish is that I would've started earlier. My advice for a new student entering the Academy is to be coachable. Be open to something that is perhaps different from what you've been doing. We can all figure things out on our own, but we only have so much time in which to make an impact in the world. People who are coachable make the biggest strides in their learning, development, and overall impact."

- AUSTIN N.

CHAPTER 14

The Golden Coaching Question

When I first knew I wanted to be a coach, there was a part of me that kept thinking, "Maybe I should wait." I thought I'd be wiser, more experienced, or maybe even more financially secure if I just held off a little bit longer. But then a new question surfaced. I kept telling myself the time wasn't right—but what if that time never actually arrived?

I imagined reaching the end of my life and looking back with regret, realizing waiting had cost me the life I truly wanted. The vision of that potential future struck me deeply. I realized I could no longer wait to start building the life I desired.

That decision was a turning point, and it all came down to one question: *"What do I want?"* This question—so simple, yet so powerful—is what I now call the golden question of coaching. And while it's a question that can open doors, it's also one of the most challenging for people to answer.

Why? Because the moment we answer it honestly, we feel the weight of responsibility to act.

For most people, this is where resistance kicks in, often in the form of thinking, "It's not the right time." For many, this belief is the single biggest barrier standing between the life they have in the present and the life they truly want.

But our dreams don't leave us alone. When we don't honor our deepest desires, we're left with a sense of unfulfillment and regret that grows over time. These dreams—the visions we carry within us—aren't supposed to feel logical or convenient. They are meant to disrupt us, to pull us out of comfort and challenge our sense of what's possible.

The Myth of the "Right Time"

One of the most persistent myths people hold is that there will someday be a "right time" to pursue their dreams. Maybe after they've paid off a bit more debt, or once they've saved enough for the future, or after the kids are older. The list goes on. While each reason may sound valid, the reality is that waiting doesn't eliminate challenges; it only reinforces the habit of deferring dreams.

The belief that it's not the right time often comes from our brain's instinct to keep us safe. The primitive part of our brains is wired to seek stability, to avoid risks, and to keep us within known limits. While this serves a purpose, it also prevents us from moving toward our highest aspirations. The "right time" is a mirage—a comforting notion that makes us feel like we're preserving control when, in fact, we're letting fear hold the reins.

Imagine someone who dreams of starting their own business but keeps putting it off, telling themselves, "I'll do it once I have more experience, once I'm financially secure, once I have more free time." They tell themselves they're being responsible, but really, they're allowing fear to dictate their choices. And if they continue down this path, they may never take that leap. They may look back one day and realize that all those "responsible" choices led them somewhere they never wanted to be. If we wait until everything is "just right," we'll wait forever.

Our visions and dreams are persistent for a reason. They're a call to action, a reminder that there's something greater within us waiting to be realized. When we don't act on what we want, we don't just let ourselves down—we also deprive the world of our unique gifts and contributions.

Our dreams aren't meant to stay hidden in our minds; they're meant to be lived.

And when we take action, even imperfect action, toward our dreams, we discover that we're capable of more than we imagined. Challenges that once seemed insurmountable start to shrink. Resources appear, opportunities unfold, and we adapt to meet the demands of the journey. This is the beauty of dreams—they shape us, push us, and ultimately expand who we are.

The Power of Starting Now

In coaching, I call this willingness to act despite uncertainty *"Vision Force."* Vision Force is the decision to pursue our dreams now, not later. It's the choice to step into our vision, even when it feels risky or inconvenient. It's about pushing through resistance and deciding, "I'm going to do this. I'm going to start now, and I'll figure it out along the way."

As a coach, one of the greatest gifts you can give your clients is the courage to embrace Vision Force. The questions below are designed to guide clients toward the ultimate golden coaching question: "What do you want?" By exploring each one, clients are encouraged to clarify their deepest desires and uncover what truly matters to them.

- What is the decision your Future Self would thank you for?
- What would be worse: pursuing your dreams and facing setbacks, or never trying at all?
- What would you do if you knew success was inevitable?
- What would you go after immediately if you didn't have to worry about failing?
- What would it look like to act on your dreams, even if life isn't 'perfectly aligned?'
- What if now was exactly the right time to start?

Life will always be busy, and there will always be distractions. If we let these distractions determine our choices, we'll never get around to what truly matters. We have to choose our dreams intentionally, with the knowledge that this is the only life we get. There's no dress rehearsal. This is our shot to create the life we want.

Creating the Life of Your Dreams

The question, "What do you want?" is not just about uncovering a wish—it's the catalyst for intentional living. When clients answer this question, they become creators in their own lives, crafting a future aligned with their values and desires.

Without clarity on what they want, clients risk living a life determined by external forces and fleeting circumstances. Just as an archer needs to see the target to hit it, your client needs a clear picture of what they want their life to look like to make it happen. Every session can circle back to this question, anchoring them in their vision and empowering them to make intentional choices.

As a coach, it's your job to help clients remember that they're the authors of their lives. They don't have to wait for permission, ideal timing, or a perfect set of circumstances. They are worth pursuing their dreams. Now and every time they choose to honor their vision, they're stepping into the life they're meant to live.

So, ask them "What do you want?" often. Keep bringing your clients back to their visions, and remind them that the right time is now. Watch as their lives unfold in ways they never thought possible.

It's always worth it to go after our dreams.

When we do, we level up. We evolve. We raise the bar for what's possible. We increase our capacity to serve, love, give, nurture, and appreciate. Every single thing in life expands as we pursue our vision.

The golden question, "What do you want?" is the guiding light that can anchor every coaching session. By continually returning to this question, you help your clients align with their truest aspirations and make choices that propel them toward their dreams. Each time they answer it honestly, they gain clarity, courage, and a renewed sense of purpose.

As you move forward, remember the coaching session is a sacred space for clients to explore this question. Your role is to hold them to that vision, encouraging them to turn their answers into action. In doing so, you empower them not just to imagine the life they desire, but to actively create it.

CHAPTER 15

The Four Flavors of Curiosity

One of the most common concerns among new coaches is *how* to ask the "right" questions. The unfortunate truth is this: there's no such thing as a perfect question. The key to effective coaching is not about knowing the right questions, but about how you approach your client with the right *flavor* of curiosity.

Think of coaching as a process of exploration. When you ask someone a question, you trigger their brain to go on a mental scavenger hunt. Depending on how you frame that question, the answers they find will either bring clarity or keep them stuck. The wording, tone, and intention behind your question influence the quality of the response.

Imagine the difference between asking someone, "Why would you do that?" versus, "I'm curious, what inspired you to make that choice?" Both questions aim to understand someone's reasoning, but each will evoke a very different response. The first may cause the client to feel defensive, while the second encourages them to explore their thought process without judgment.

As a coach, understanding the flavors of curiosity you bring into your sessions can transform the way your clients open up and engage with their challenges. There are four primary types of curiosity you may encounter: judgmental curiosity, disorganized curiosity, biased curiosity, and neutral curiosity. The following is a breakdown of how each type influences the coaching dynamic.

1. Judgmental Curiosity: A Barrier to Trust

Judgmental curiosity comes from a place of assuming there's something wrong with the client or their choices. When you approach with judgmental curiosity, you're likely asking questions that provoke defensiveness, which creates distance between you and your client. These types of questions often sound like:

- What's wrong with you?
- Why would you do that?
- Why didn't you follow through?

The problem with judgmental questions is that they suggest something is inherently flawed in the client's actions, thoughts, or feelings. When someone feels judged, they're less likely to engage openly and honestly. Instead, they may feel the need to defend themselves, which shuts down the potential for self-awareness and insight. This barrier makes it harder for your client to explore their underlying motivations and fears, limiting the effectiveness of the session.

If a client has been procrastinating on a key goal, asking them, "Why haven't you done it yet?" immediately puts them on the defensive. Instead, a non-judgmental approach might sound like, "I'm curious, what's been coming up for you when you think about starting this project?" This encourages the client to explore their own barriers without feeling attacked.

2. Disorganized Curiosity: A Roadblock to Focus

Disorganized curiosity occurs when a coach asks questions that seem irrelevant or scattered, leading the conversation in multiple directions without contributing to the client's goals. You might be gathering information, but it's not helping the client gain clarity or progress.

For example, imagine a client shares they felt frustrated because a police officer gave them a speeding ticket earlier that day. Disorganized questions might sound like:

- How fast were you driving?
- What was the weather like that day?
- Was the officer rude or polite?

These questions may satisfy your own curiosity, but they don't help the client reflect on the root cause of the issue or move forward. While these details may be interesting, they're ultimately distractions. This scattered approach can make the coaching session feel unfocused, leaving the client frustrated and uncertain about how to proceed.

Effective coaching requires honing in on the client's primary challenge. In this scenario, a more empowering question might be, "When you were given the ticket, what story did you tell yourself?" or "What assumption is fueling your frustration?" Questions like these help the client deepen their self-awareness and stay aligned with the session's purpose.

3. Biased Curiosity: A Threat to Client Autonomy

Biased curiosity takes place when the coach subtly guides the client toward a particular answer or outcome. This type of questioning often comes from the coach's own assumptions or ideas about what the client *should* do. Biased curiosity might sound like:

- Have you considered trying X?
- What if you did it this way instead?
- Wouldn't you agree that Y could be the right next step?

On the surface, these questions may seem helpful, but they can undermine the client's autonomy and suggest that the coach has the "right" answer. This can make the client feel pressured to conform to the coach's advice rather than exploring their own unique insights. Ultimately, biased questions prevent the client from tapping into their own inner wisdom and finding the solutions that resonate most with them.

Effective coaching avoids imposing solutions and instead empowers the client to come up with their own. For example, if a client is struggling with time management, rather than saying, "What if you used a time-blocking technique?" you could ask, "What strategies have worked for you in the past to manage your time more effectively?" This allows the client to reflect on their own experiences and build solutions that align with their strengths and preferences.

4. Neutral Curiosity: The Key to Insight and Exploration

The most powerful form of curiosity in coaching is neutral curiosity. Neutral curiosity involves asking open-ended, unbiased questions that invite the client to explore their thoughts, feelings, and experiences without judgment or direction. This type of questioning creates a safe space for clients to reflect deeply and discover new insights.

Neutral questions are designed to clarify, not to lead or critique. They invite the client into a deeper conversation with themselves. They are designed to clarify and encourage exploration. For instance:

- What's your perspective on this situation?
- What would an ideal outcome look like?
- How did that experience impact you?
- What possibilities do you see here?
- What are you noticing right now?
- How did you come to that conclusion?
- What's another perspective you could consider?
- How does this idea fit in with your values?
- What is your gut telling you right now?
- What can you learn from this experience?
- What's the most meaningful action you can take right now?

These types of questions invite the client to dive deeper into their own experiences without feeling pressured to give a particular answer. Neutral curiosity signals to the client that their thoughts and emotions are valid, creating an atmosphere of trust and openness. This is where true breakthroughs happen—when clients feel supported in exploring their own truth.

Notice how these questions encourage the client to reflect, without imposing any opinion from the coach. They are neither leading nor judgmental. They simply open the door for the client to explore more deeply.

Imagine a client who is unsure about a major career decision. Instead of asking, "Have you thought about staying in your current role for a bit longer?" (which leads them toward a specific outcome), a neutral question could be, "What does your gut tell you about this decision?" This shifts the focus back onto the client's inner wisdom, allowing them to explore without external influence.

Neutral curiosity is where the magic of coaching happens. By staying curious without bias, you create a safe and supportive space for your client to dig deeper into their own thoughts and find clarity. You're not there to give them the answers—you're there to help them uncover their own.

In the chart below, you'll find three scenarios along with examples of how each flavor of curiosity might sound.

Scenario	Judgmental Curiosity	Disorganized Curiosity	Biased Curiosity	Neutral Curiosity
Client struggling with a career decision	Why are you still at that job if you're unhappy?	What was your first job? Who was your boss there? How long did you work there?	Have you thought about looking for a job in a different field?	What about your current job makes you feel unhappy? How would you like to explore this in our session?
Client dealing with relationship issues	Why can't you just move on from your ex?	How did you meet your ex? What was your first date like? Have you contacted them recently?	What if your ex is not the right person for you? Have you considered dating someone new?	When you think about reaching out to your ex, what feelings come up? What would you like to achieve by reconnecting?
Client facing a health challenge	Why haven't you stuck to your health plan?	What did you eat yesterday? How much did you exercise last week? What time do you go to bed?	What if you tried a different diet or exercise routine?	Can you tell me more about the challenges you're facing with your health plan? What goals do you want to achieve regarding your health?

Mastering the art of asking questions doesn't happen overnight. It's a skill that develops over time as you practice and refine your approach. Start by becoming more aware of the types of curiosity you bring into your sessions. Notice if your questions come from a place of judgment, distraction, bias, or neutrality. With practice, you'll learn to ask questions that open up conversation rather than close it down.

When you make the shift to neutral curiosity, you'll see a profound difference in your coaching. Your clients will feel more supported, and they'll be more willing to explore their thoughts and feelings openly. In turn, this will lead to more meaningful progress and deeper insights.

The next time you're in a session and wondering what to ask, remember: there's no perfect question. Focus instead on bringing the right flavor of curiosity, and the answers will follow.

Special Gift

To make your coaching sessions even more impactful, I'm offering you a free resource: 50+ Empowering Questions you can use with your clients. These questions are designed to inspire deeper insights and breakthroughs in your sessions.

To access your gift, simply scan the QR code below or visit

www.thrivingcoachacademy.com/questions

CHAPTER 16

Transformational Listening

n my early coaching career, I encountered a client who was a mother and entrepreneur on the cusp of turning fifty. She came to me seeking guidance to envision the next decade of her life, brimming with dreams yet uncertain about her path forward. As we began our sessions, I found myself wondering—what questions should I ask? Instead of forcing the dialogue, I chose to simply listen.

To my surprise, at the end of each session, she would express heartfelt gratitude, saying, "This was so helpful! You are an amazing coach. Thank you!" Each time, I was left feeling as if I had done little to earn such praise. It wasn't until a few sessions in that I realized how powerful listening alone could be, even though it is often underrated.

Listening isn't passive; it's an active way to connect with clients, giving them a safe space to explore their thoughts and feelings. It's something you have to practice and continually refine. When I listened closely and paid attention, I gave this client the gift of feeling heard and understood. This realization transformed my understanding of coaching, showing me that the art of listening is, in fact, a powerful skill.

The Power of Listening in Coaching

True listening extends beyond hearing words—it's about grasping the essence of the individual in front of you. In a world where people rarely feel fully listened to, the ability to listen with focus can set you apart as a coach and provide great value to clients.

To help you navigate this journey, let's explore the five levels of listening, each representing a deeper connection and engagement with your client:

1. **Ignoring**. The first level is marked by a complete lack of attention. This often happens when distractions, such as phones or racing thoughts, pull the listener away from the conversation. Ignoring conveys a powerful message: the speaker's words do not hold value. In coaching, this kind of listening breaks trust and blocks progress. Important details about a client's needs and concerns can be easily missed.

Example:
Client: I've been feeling really stressed lately.
Coach: (Distracted) Sorry, could you repeat that?

2. **Pretending**. At this stage, the listener may nod or say "uh-huh," but they aren't truly engaged. This superficial engagement might lead clients to feel undervalued, as their concerns are not genuinely heard. Pretending often leads to misunderstandings and frustration.

Example:
Client: I'm unsure what direction to take in my career.
Coach: Uh-huh, I see.

3. **Subjective**. Subjective listening occurs when the listener hears the speaker's words but interprets them through their own experiences. While this can create a false sense of connection, it often diverts attention from the speaker's needs, preventing deeper understanding.

Example:
Client: I'm struggling to balance work and family.
Coach: Yeah, I had the same issue last year. Here's what I did...

4. **Objective**. At this level, the listener paraphrases what the speaker shares to ensure clarity and understanding. This builds real engagement and empathy.

Example:
Client: I feel like I'm constantly failing at my job. My manager keeps giving me negative feedback, and I'm starting to doubt my abilities.
Coach: So, what I'm hearing is that the negative feedback is causing you to doubt your abilities. Is that correct?

5. **Transformational**. The highest level of listening, transformational listening, transcends words. It involves tuning into unspoken concerns and sensing shifts in tone, energy, and body language. This deep level of listening captures the essence of the individual, allowing for transformative breakthroughs.

   Example:
   Coach: I notice a shift in your tone when discussing your job. It seems like there's a deeper concern there. Can we explore that?
   Client: I keep procrastinating on important tasks.
   Coach: I sense there might be an underlying fear of failure driving this procrastination. Let's delve into what's truly holding you back.

As coaches, we should aim for at least Level 4: Objective Listening to genuinely connect with and understand our clients. However, striving for Level 5: Transformational Listening can lead to profound insights and lasting change.

By understanding and practicing these listening levels, we can improve our coaching skills and guide clients to have breakthroughs.

The Language of Self-Sabotage

Language plays a pivotal role in the journey of personal transformation. As a coach, your success relies not only on comprehending your clients' words but also on your ability to listen deeply to how they articulate their challenges and aspirations. Subtle nuances in their speech can either empower them or reinforce self-limiting beliefs.

For example, consider a client who repeatedly says, "I can't," or, "I'm not good enough." These phrases reflect deeper beliefs that impede their growth. Through attentive listening, you can identify these patterns and gently challenge them, guiding clients to replace limiting language with empowering alternatives.

One common language pattern I notice in clients is the use of "should," "have to," and "but." These words often indicate a mindset of self-sabotage, creating mental barriers that keep clients from pursuing their goals.

1. **Should** often signifies an external expectation or obligation. This word can create feelings of guilt or inadequacy. For instance, a client might say, "I should be further along in my career by now." By emphasizing this word, they impose a sense of failure on themselves, which can be paralyzing. A better approach could be to ask, "What would happen if you focused on your progress instead of comparing yourself to others?"

2. **Have to** often reflects a sense of coercion, suggesting that the client feels trapped by their circumstances. A client may express, "I have to attend this networking event, even though I'm not comfortable." This language reinforces a lack of agency, making clients feel as though they are being forced into situations. Instead, encourage clients to shift their perspective. "How can you view this networking opportunity as a *want to* instead of a *have to*?"

3. **But** introduces a contradiction that undermines positive affirmations. For example, a client might say, "I want to start my own business, but I'm afraid of failing." The "but" diminishes their aspirations and reinforces fear.

Encourage clients to reframe their language so they say something like, "I want to start my own business, and I can explore ways to manage my fear." This shift fosters a sense of empowerment and possibility.

As coaches, it's essential to help clients spot and change self-sabotaging language. This helps them break free from limiting beliefs and adopt a more empowered mindset.

Transformational listening is not merely a technique; it is a cornerstone of impactful coaching. It demands intention, attention, and a commitment to engage with clients at a profound level. By mastering the various levels of listening and recognizing the influence of language, you can guide your clients toward meaningful insights and lasting transformation.

As you hone your listening skills and foster awareness of self-sabotaging language, you'll create an environment where breakthroughs flourish, allowing clients to step confidently into their desired futures.

CHAPTER 17

Other People's Opinions

As a coach, one of the biggest obstacles your clients will face is fear—most usually, fear of how others will react to their goals and dreams. People naturally worry about what others think, and this fear often holds them back from pursuing their true desires. In your coaching practice, it's essential to help clients overcome this challenge because until they release the grip of other people's opinions, they'll struggle to move forward confidently.

Judgment is unavoidable. People will judge you no matter what path you take in life. They will judge you whether you are playing big or small. Rather than trying to escape the judgment of others, you get to decide what version of you you want people to judge.

> *Do you want people to judge the version of you that is authentic and sharing your gifts with the world, or the version of you that is playing small and hiding?*

People have the freedom to judge. They have the freedom to agree or disagree with you. You don't have control over people's judgments. But you do have control over living in alignment with who you are. You need to decide what's more important to you: avoiding other people's judgment or transforming people's lives.

Understanding Whose Opinion Matters

When we put ourselves out there—whether in our personal lives, careers, or relationships—people will have opinions. They'll critique how we talk, dress, eat, spend money, and pursue our dreams. It's easy for clients to fall into the trap of seeking approval or validation from others, but as a coach, your role is to help them realize that what truly matters is *their* opinion of themselves.

Recently, I mentored a highly successful coach who was earning well into the six figures. Despite her financial success, she was worried that speaking her mind would lead to criticism. I asked her a simple question: "What is your opinion of you?" After a long pause, she admitted she'd never considered it.

Like many people, she had spent years relying on external feedback to shape her self-worth. Most people do not consider their opinion of themselves. Instead, they rely on other people's opinions of them. When my client realized this, it was a huge breakthrough for her because she started to examine that question and create her opinion of herself for the first time.

She said, "I care about people. I know I have value to offer. I know I'm here to make a difference. I'm a person who reaches her goals. I'm disciplined."

The more clients build their own sense of self, the less they'll care about what others think. Your job is to guide them in developing an unshakable inner confidence, rooted in their values, abilities, and purpose. When they learn to answer the question, *"Who am I?"* with clarity and conviction, other people's opinions will hold less weight.

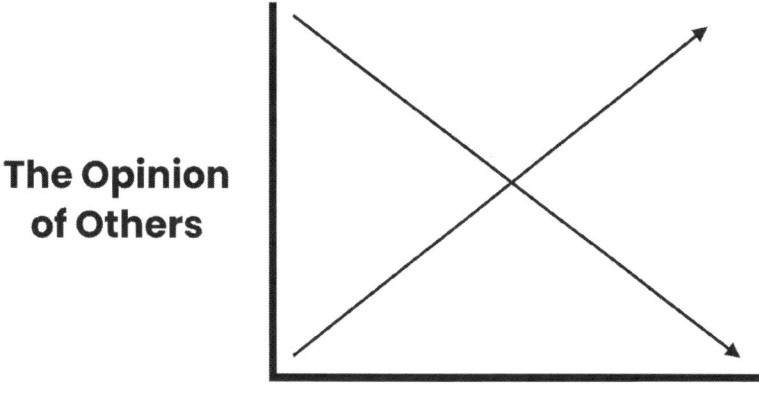

The Opinion of Others

Your Opinion of You

The Illusion of Judgment: It's Not About You

It's important to help clients understand that other people's opinions aren't necessarily about them. When someone judges you, they're really expressing something about themselves—about their own values, experiences, and biases. Their opinion says more about who they are than who you are.

For example, if someone calls you "selfish" or "bossy," it likely reflects their own discomfort with assertiveness or unmet needs rather than any inherent truth about you. Their words reveal how they view the world and what behaviors they find challenging or triggering.

It only affects you if you believe it's true. Think of it like this: if someone told me, "I hate your blue hair," I wouldn't feel defensive at all—because I know I don't have blue hair. Their comment has no power because it doesn't align with the truth I know about myself. This same principle applies when people criticize you. If you are clear about who you are, you won't be shaken by their judgments.

But what if their criticism is about something true? Even then, it's important to remember that their judgment is still shaped by their own perspectives, values, and biases. For example, if you do have blue hair and someone says they hate it, that opinion reflects their personal preferences—it doesn't make blue hair inherently bad or wrong. What matters most is how you feel about it. If you love your blue hair, their comment doesn't have to affect your confidence or self-worth.

Some might wonder, "Does this mean I should just ignore everyone's criticism?" Not at all. The goal isn't to dismiss all feedback but to evaluate it thoughtfully. Criticism can sometimes offer valuable insights, especially when it comes from a trusted source or is delivered constructively.

However, the key is to distinguish between helpful feedback and opinions that don't serve you. Helpful criticism is rooted in care and invites growth, while unhelpful judgment often reflects the other person's biases or insecurities. Encourage clients to ask themselves, "Is this criticism coming from someone I trust and respect? Does it help me grow or align more closely with my values?" If the answer is no, it's okay to let it go.

For clients, this realization is liberating. Their work isn't to convince everyone to like them. Instead, their work is to become at peace with the fact that some people won't like them—and that's okay.

Surrounding Yourself with the Right People

As clients step into their potential, they will inevitably encounter people who are threatened by their growth. Some may say, "You've changed," or "You're too much," in an attempt to hold them back. This is why it's crucial to help clients surround themselves with people who support both the person they are now and the person they are becoming.

Remind them that no matter how noble, kind, or generous they try to be, there will always be people who don't like them. You could be the juiciest peach on the tree, but some people just don't like peaches. Trying to please everyone is a recipe for frustration and burnout. Instead, help them focus on finding their inner circle—the people who uplift, inspire, and encourage them to keep growing.

It's also important to remind clients that *they will never be criticized by someone doing more than them*. People who are truly successful and fulfilled are too busy living their own lives to criticize others. It's often those who feel insecure or threatened that project their judgments onto others. As a coach, you can help clients develop the mindset that the opinions of those doing less or living smaller should not hold them back.

Owning Your Life and Letting Others Down

Sometimes, in order to lift yourself up, you must let others down. This might mean disappointing people who want you to stay in your comfort zone or follow a more traditional path. But the reality is, living for other people's expectations only leads to resentment and regret. Ask your clients, *"Who are you living for?"* Are you making choices based on what you truly want, or are you living for someone else's approval?

This is especially important when it comes to starting a coaching business. Your clients won't gain anything from asking for opinions from people who don't understand the coaching industry or who don't share their vision. Encourage them to focus on their goals and to seek guidance only from those who have walked the path they want to follow.

Lastly, remind clients that *it's not their business what other people think of them*. What truly matters is staying aligned with your own values and staying true to who you are. When clients can grasp this, they'll find that other people's opinions—good or bad—start to lose their hold.

As a coach, your role is to help clients develop an unshakable sense of self-worth that isn't dependent on the opinions of others. Help them realize that what people say is about *them*, but what they hear is about *themselves*. By teaching them to reinterpret judgment and stand confidently in their truth, you will empower them to pursue their dreams with freedom, confidence, and resilience.

CHAPTER 18

Choosing Your Failure

I n the first few years of growing my coaching business, I had a moment when I questioned if I should really continue. It was hard. I was struggling, dealing with rejection, and wondering if I was truly cut out for this path. Every potential client that said "no," every email that went unanswered, and every slow month felt like a failure, chipping away at my confidence.

There was a moment when I sat down and seriously considered walking away. I thought about what life would look like if I gave up on my dream. I knew I could go back to a stable job—a job that might offer me security, a steady paycheck, and outward success.

But then I imagined myself in that life—working long hours at a job that didn't fulfill me, day after day, year after year. I pictured the dread of waking up every morning, knowing that my efforts were serving someone else's vision, not my own. The thought of being stuck in meetings that drained my energy, doing tasks that had no real meaning to me, and constantly feeling the weight of someone else's expectations was suffocating.

I knew that over time, this would eat away at my spirit. Even if I had a nice paycheck and looked successful on the outside, I knew that inside, I would feel disconnected and empty.

That vision gave me perspective. I realized I would much rather face the setbacks of building my coaching business—rejections, slow months, and challenges—than live with the deep regret of never having tried to create something of my own. The pain of temporary failure was nothing compared to the lifelong regret of working for someone else and never following my true purpose.

That's when it hit me: failure comes in two forms. It's not about "How can I avoid failure?" because no matter what path I chose, failure was inevitable. The real question became, "Which failure do I want to choose?" Do I want the failure of falling short while pursuing my passion? Or do I want the failure of living a life that wasn't mine, driven by external validation but lacking true fulfillment?

Once I saw the choice clearly, I knew I wanted to continue on my coaching path. The struggles I faced weren't signs that I was failing—they were signs that I was moving toward something greater, toward a life that aligned with my deepest desires. That moment redefined failure for me, and it's a lesson I've carried into every aspect of my coaching practice.

As a transformational coach, you'll encounter many clients who, like I was, are paralyzed by the fear of failure. But the truth is, no matter what path we take in life, failure is inevitable. There is no avoiding it. It's not a question of whether you will fail, but how you will fail. And more importantly, which failure we will choose.

Your role as a coach is to help your clients understand that failure isn't something to avoid—it's something to confront head-on. In fact, the only real choice we have when it comes to failure is whether we'll experience Good Failure or Bad Failure.

Good Failure: Outward Failure and Inward Success

Good Failure is the path that may be filled with setbacks but leads to growth, meaning, and a life lived authentically. Good Failure is the kind of failure you want your clients to experience because it is the failure of trying—of stepping out of their comfort zone and daring to pursue their dreams. It's the type of failure that moves them closer to success, even when it feels like a setback.

This type of failure occurs when your client pursues something they truly want but experiences challenges along the way. On the outside, they may face rejection, criticism, or even financial loss. However, inwardly, they succeed because they are living in alignment with their deepest desires.

Consider a client who starts their own business that doesn't gain traction right away. From the outside, it may look like they've failed. But in reality, they've succeeded because they're following their passion and learning valuable lessons along the way. What's crucial is that their failures are not signs of defeat but markers of progress.

Take Thomas Edison's story, for example. He famously said, "I have not failed. I've just found 10,000 ways that won't work." Each failure brought him closer to success, illustrating that failure can be a step forward rather than a step back. Good Failure means having the willingness to keep moving despite setbacks, knowing that each "failure" is a part of the process.

Questions to Reflect on Good Failure

To help your clients embrace Good Failure and turn setbacks into opportunities for growth, consider encouraging them to reflect on the following questions:

1. What is the lesson you can learn from this failure?

2. How can you reframe this failure as a stepping stone to success?

3. What does this failure teach you about your purpose?

4. Who can you reach out to for support and encouragement during this time?

5. In what ways have you grown or changed because of this experience?

Bad Failure: Inward Failure and Outward Success

Bad Failure happens when someone achieves outward success but feels empty on the inside. They may be climbing the corporate ladder, accumulating wealth, or receiving praise from others, but they feel unfulfilled because they've compromised their dreams for external validation. Bad Failure is more insidious than Good Failure because it gives the appearance of success while leaving someone internally disconnected from their true purpose.

While Good Failure involves pain and struggle in pursuit of something meaningful, Bad Failure is the quiet suffering of living a life that doesn't align with who you are. It's the failure of choosing safety over authenticity, of prioritizing others' expectations over your own desires. The pain of Bad Failure isn't immediate, but it's long-lasting—it's the pain of regret.

Questions to Reflect on Bad Failure

To help your clients recognize and navigate Bad Failure, encourage them to ask themselves these reflective questions:

1. Are you living a life true to yourself, or are you trying to meet others' expectations?

2. What sacrifices are you making for the sake of success, and are they worth it?

3. How does your current path align with your passions and interests?

4. What feelings of emptiness or dissatisfaction are you experiencing?

5. What steps can you take to reconnect with your authentic self and desires?

By guiding your clients through these reflections, you empower them to make conscious choices about the kind of failure they experience. With this understanding, they can move forward with courage, ready to embrace the journey ahead.

CHAPTER 19

Trusting the Coaching Process

A s a coach, it's natural to experience moments of doubt and uncertainty. You might question whether your clients are genuinely benefiting from your sessions, or feel unsure about the direction you're taking during the coaching process. Perhaps you even second-guess your own techniques, wondering if you're using the "right" approach.

These concerns can feel overwhelming, and can lead you to question your competence and the value you bring to the table. In fact, nearly every coach—whether seasoned or new—experiences these doubts at some point. What separates those who thrive from those who flounder is the ability to confront these fears head-on and embrace the inherent unpredictability of the coaching process. After all, the true power of coaching lies in the journey, not just the destination.

In this chapter, we'll address three common concerns that many coaches face:

- I feel lost in my sessions.
- My client didn't experience a breakthrough (so I believe they didn't receive value).
- I didn't use the right coaching tool.

Each of these concerns can weigh heavily on you, but by learning how to navigate them, you can transform your approach to coaching and find renewed confidence in the process.

"I Feel Lost in My Sessions."

Have you ever felt completely lost during a coaching session? It's a disconcerting feeling—one that can fill you with doubt, anxiety, and even panic. But what if being "lost" wasn't something to fear, but something to embrace?

The first time I traveled to Italy, I arrived in Rome with no itinerary, no map, and no specific destination in mind. After checking into my small hotel, I simply set out to wander the streets of Rome. I strolled through narrow cobblestone alleys, admiring the vibrant colors of the buildings and listening to the lively chatter of locals. I had no clue where I was going, yet I felt an overwhelming sense of freedom. I was lost, but in a good way—exploring without fear, letting the experience unfold naturally.

In that moment, I realized a profound truth: you cannot be lost when you are exploring. As a coach, this mindset can revolutionize your sessions. Coaching is not about having all the answers or leading your client to a predetermined destination. It's about exploration—discovering new insights, paths, and possibilities with your client. When you shift your perspective from being "lost" to being an explorer, the fear dissolves. Exploration brings curiosity, openness, and excitement.

Next time you feel lost in a session, ask yourself, "Am I really lost, or am I exploring?" By framing your experience as an adventure of discovery rather than a mistake, you open yourself up to new possibilities. This shift in mindset can make all the difference. Your role as a coach isn't to have all the answers but to create a space where your client can uncover their own. The magic happens in the exploration.

"My Client Didn't Experience a Breakthrough."

Coaches often equate value with breakthroughs—those "aha" moments when a client experiences a sudden, life-altering realization. While breakthroughs are exhilarating, they are not the only measure of value in coaching. In fact, focusing solely on breakthroughs can leave both you and your client feeling frustrated if one doesn't occur.

Not every session will produce fireworks, and that's okay. The value of coaching can manifest in small, subtle shifts—tiny insights that build upon each other over time. Just because a client didn't have a dramatic breakthrough doesn't mean they didn't gain something meaningful from the session. Growth is often gradual, like planting seeds that will bloom later.

Think of coaching like a long journey. Some days, progress is visible and significant; other days, it's quiet and reflective. Both types of sessions serve a purpose. Clients might leave a session without a clear breakthrough but still benefit from the space you provided for them to reflect, process, and think more deeply. Sometimes, a single question or insight may spark a transformation later on, when they least expect it.

One powerful way to affirm the value of your sessions is to ask clients directly, "What value did you get from our session today?" This question prompts reflection and can reveal unexpected takeaways. Sometimes, clients will articulate the benefits of a session in ways you hadn't anticipated, reinforcing your role in their growth.

The next time you worry that your client didn't receive value because there wasn't a major shift, remind yourself that progress can be incremental. Trust the process, and celebrate the small victories along the way.

"I Didn't Use the Right Coaching Tool."

As coaches, we often feel pressure to use the "right" tool or technique in every session. When a session doesn't go as planned, it's easy to second-guess ourselves. "Should I have tried a different approach?" or, "Did I pick the wrong tool?"

The truth is, there is no one-size-fits-all tool in coaching. Every client is different, and every session has its own rhythm. What works brilliantly with one client may fall flat with another—and that's perfectly normal. The key is adaptability, not perfection.

Think of coaching as a journey up a mountain. There are multiple trails to the summit, each with its own unique challenge and scenery. Similarly, there are many ways to guide a client from point A to point B. If one approach doesn't work, that doesn't mean it was wrong; it simply means there may be another path to explore.

Doctors face similar challenges when prescribing treatments. Not every medication works the same for every patient. Sometimes, they have to try multiple options before finding the right fit. This doesn't mean the doctor is ineffective; it just means that trial and error are part of the process. In coaching, the same principle applies.

If you ever doubt whether you used the "right" tool, ask yourself, "Did I approach this session with curiosity and a genuine desire to help?" If the answer is yes, trust that you gave your best. Coaching is an art, not a formula, and it's okay to experiment and adapt. Just as there are many paths to success, there are many coaching tools that can guide a client toward their goals.

Embracing the Coaching Journey

Ultimately, the journey of coaching is about continuous exploration and growth—for both you and your clients. There will be moments of doubt, confusion, and uncertainty, but those moments don't define your effectiveness as a coach. Instead, they offer opportunities to deepen your practice, embrace curiosity, and trust the process.

When you feel lost, remind yourself that exploration is where discovery happens. When breakthroughs are absent, remember that growth is a gradual process. And when a tool doesn't work, see it as an invitation to experiment, adapt, and refine.

The coaching journey is rich with opportunities to learn, evolve, and make a meaningful impact on your clients' lives. Trust in that journey, and you'll find that both you and your clients are exactly where you need to be.

CHAPTER 20

Finishing Sessions Strong

The same year I became a coach, I heard about vision boards. The idea was simple: grab a stack of magazines, cut out pictures that represent your dreams, and arrange them on a board. The promise? That by simply placing these images in front of me, I could "manifest" my dreams into reality. So, I dove in and spent hours gathering photos, arranging them, and creating a beautiful, vivid picture of my ideal future. I covered my board with images of countries I wanted to explore, symbols of financial freedom, and snapshots representing the kind of relationship I dreamed of attracting.

But as I finished, it dawned on me that the board itself wouldn't magically manifest anything. Sure, it represented my goals and desires, but without real effort and consistent action, those images would remain just that—images. If I wanted to turn them into reality, I still had to make them happen. The vision board was just the start.

You cannot manifest anything without first taking action. As a coach, it's your responsibility to support your clients in pairing their insights with purposeful action steps. It's not enough to simply imagine a goal or even to have an inspiring "aha" moment. This is the purpose of the end of a coaching session.

Clarifying the Action Step

The action step at the end of each session is crucial because it moves the client from "knowing" to "doing." For an action step to be effective, it must be clear, specific, and active. Below are some tips for navigating the end of a session.

1. **Use Guiding Questions to Define the Action**
   Questions like these help the client think critically about what they can do, making the action step clear and purposeful:
   • What's one way you can take your insight from today and put it into action?
   • How can you apply what we uncovered in this session?

- What's one specific thing you can do this week to move closer to your goal?
- What's one activity that challenges you and would help you build on today's insights?

2. Be Specific

A vague action step like "exercise" or "work on self-confidence" won't drive change. Instead, encourage your client to identify a precise action that's easy to understand and track. For example, if your client's goal is to build confidence, a specific action might be "introduce myself to one new person at the office." Or, if they want to improve fitness, it could be "attend one group exercise class this week." Specificity keeps the action step grounded and eliminates any ambiguity about what your client needs to do.

3. Ensure the Action is Active, Not Passive

Passive steps, such as "reflect" or "meditate," can still be helpful—but they may lack the stretch necessary to drive change. Instead, an action step should be active and demand a degree of effort or engagement. When a client chooses something that stretches them, it helps them break out of their comfort zone and build new skills or behaviors. For example, rather than "reflect on confidence," a client might decide to "give a brief presentation at work to practice confidence." This kind of active step promotes growth through real-world practice.

Encouraging Commitment Through Accountability

An action step is most effective when it's more than a mere suggestion—it's a commitment. By helping clients set up accountability, you add a form of positive pressure that supports their success. Just as it takes pressure to make a rock into a diamond, accountability can encourage a client to rise to their potential.

Here are a few ways clients can hold themselves accountable to their action steps:

- **Set Deadlines.** A clear timeline can be motivating and adds a sense of urgency. Encourage clients to commit to a specific deadline, such as "by next Tuesday," rather than a vague "sometime next week." Setting a timeframe makes the action step feel real and actionable.

- **Tell Someone Else.** Another way to add accountability is for the client to share their action step with someone they trust—a friend, family member, or even you, their coach. Knowing someone else is aware of their commitment provides an added incentive to follow through. People are often more likely to stay committed when they know others are expecting them to deliver.

- **Create a Tracking Method.** Suggest that clients use a journal, app, or other tracking method to monitor their progress. Tracking their actions can provide a sense of accomplishment and help them see tangible results, reinforcing their motivation to keep going.

These accountability strategies not only encourage commitment but also empower clients to build self-discipline and consistency. Knowing they have accountability gives clients a greater sense of responsibility and increases their likelihood of taking action, which is essential for progress.

Why Action Matters: Dreamers vs. Doers

It's largely believed there are two types of people in the world: dreamers and doers. Dreamers are those who talk about their big ideas but rarely follow through. They're full of plans to start a business, write a book, or make a major life change, yet those dreams rarely turn into reality. Dreamers spend a lot of time in "idea land," where things feel exciting but are ultimately only imagined.

Then there are doers. Doers are the ones who bridge the gap between ideas and reality. They act, learn, grow, and sometimes fail, but they keep going. Doers are the ones who move forward even when things feel uncomfortable or imperfect. They understand that real change and growth happen outside their comfort zones. And the difference? Doers take action.

By helping your client define an action step, you invite them to be a doer. This is where clients begin seeing tangible results and where real transformation starts. By ending each session with a defined action step, you set clients up with purpose and direction, equipped to make real, meaningful changes in their lives.

We've now covered how to guide your clients through transformational sessions. You've learned how to help them move toward their dreams, use curiosity and active listening to unlock deeper insights, and empower them to create lasting change with clear, actionable steps.

In the next section, we'll dive into what it takes to launch your own coaching business. Get ready to turn your coaching skills into a rewarding career.

TOP 10 INSIGHTS

1. The golden coaching question, "What do you most want?", is essential to uncovering clients' desires and serves as the foundation for intentional living.

2. There will never be a "perfect time" to pursue your goals; the key is to start now, regardless of the circumstances.

3. The quality of your curiosity shapes coaching sessions— neutral curiosity creates space for insight without leading them or becoming entangled in their story.

4. The most transformational listening involves tuning into unspoken Rules, emotions, and energy.

5. Helping clients reframe self-sabotaging language, such as "I can't" or "I should," empowers them to rewrite Old Rules and take meaningful action.

6. Releasing the fear of judgment allows clients to confidently pursue their goals, living authentically without being held back by others' opinions.

7. Encouraging clients to develop a strong opinion of themselves based on their values and purpose leads to greater self-confidence and clarity.

8. The greatest mistake in life is avoiding "good failure," where setbacks lead to growth, and instead settling for "bad failure," living a life misaligned with your true purpose.

9. You'll never feel lost in a session when you instead see it as an opportunity to explore.

10. It's crucial to help clients set clear, actionable steps and hold them accountable for making progress toward their goals.

Launching Your Coaching Business

"I discovered coaching a couple years ago. As a stage designer in Germany, I had passion for my job, but I didn't enjoy my work environment. I had this wish that my life would change completely. Within a couple months of enrolling in Thriving Coach Academy, things started skyrocketing. I felt so much confidence in coaching that I decided to quit my job and be a full-time coach. My mind was telling me 'you're not ready' and, 'you're not good enough,' but with the coaching of Frank and his team, I got to the point that I just did it. I never imagined it to happen so quickly. I love knowing the skill of coaching and having the possibility to enjoy my work. The program really changed my life on every level. I'm glad that I decided to just do it."

- SINA G.

CHAPTER 21

Unleashing Your Inner Entrepreneur

I still remember the first time I considered entrepreneurship. One evening, while scrolling through a blog, I stumbled upon a phrase that resonated deeply with me: *"Live on your own terms."* Those words awakened a passion for entrepreneurship I hadn't fully recognized within myself.

The idea of living on my own terms spoke to a longing I had buried under the expectations of a traditional path. Up until then, I had been following the "safe" route—school, career, paycheck—yet it always felt like something was missing. That phrase struck a chord because it offered the possibility of freely building a life that reflected my true values and aspirations, rather than someone else's definition of success. Suddenly, the conventional paths I'd been following felt inadequate.

Why conform to a predefined version of success when I could carve my own path? That night, I couldn't stop thinking about what it would mean to be my own boss. But even as excitement surged through me, I was also grappling with doubts. *Am I really cut out for this? Do I have what it takes to run my own business?*

Entrepreneurship isn't reserved for a select few. It's not about luck or having a particular personality. It's not about being extroverted, having high energy, or building a vast network. It's also not about automatically knowing all the ins and outs of running a business.

Most people aren't raised to understand how to run a business—instead, we're taught how to be good employees, follow instructions, and stick to a well-defined path. Entrepreneurship, on the contrary, requires learning how to navigate uncertainty, take ownership of your growth, and master skills like marketing, sales, and business strategy.

But the good news is, all of this is *learnable*, and it's a lot simpler than you may think.

This is where the Success Triangle comes into play. The triangle consists of three essential components that will guarantee you a successful coaching practice: frameworks, mentorship, and community. These three pillars are the foundation of any thriving business.

The Success Triangle

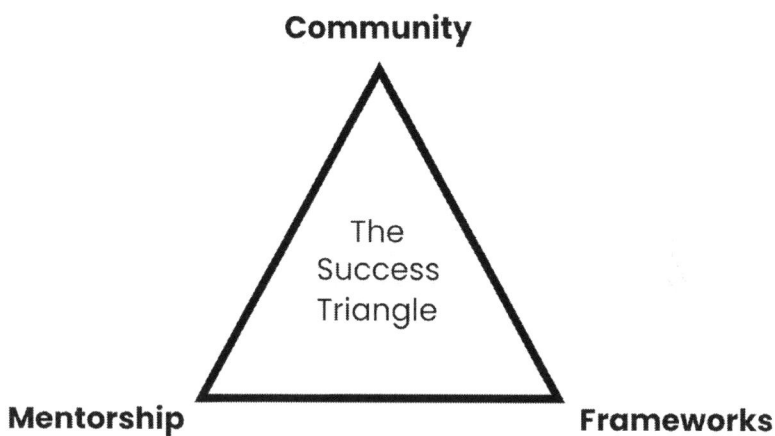

1. **Frameworks**: The "How-To" of Success

If you were lost in a forest and someone handed you a map, wouldn't you take it? Frameworks are that map. They save you time and energy by guiding you down a proven path, rather than leaving you to wander aimlessly, hoping things will work out.

Frameworks provide the essential knowledge needed to navigate entrepreneurship successfully. By reading this book, you're already accessing frameworks designed to help you succeed. In this section and the final part of the book, I'll show you how to set up a Premium Business Model—a framework for building a six- and seven-figure coaching business.

Of the three parts of the Success Triangle, frameworks are the easiest to access. The bad news? While knowledge is essential, information alone won't transform your life or business. If it could, everyone would already be thriving given how much information is available today.

Take weight loss, for example. Someone may know the importance of exercise intellectually, but still struggle to commit to a fitness routine. That's why the other two legs of the Success Triangle—mentorship and community—are equally critical.

2. Mentorship: No One Becomes Successful Alone

The myth of the "solo-preneur" is just that—a myth. Behind every successful entrepreneur is a mentor offering the guidance, accountability, and support necessary to thrive. A mentor helps you navigate challenges, avoid common pitfalls, and stay focused on your goals. Without mentorship, it's easy to lose direction or become overwhelmed—but with it, the path to success becomes clearer and more achievable.

Just as a sports coach helps athletes reach their full potential, a mentor provides invaluable insights, encouragement, and feedback, helping you overcome obstacles and remain on track. A mentor is an extra set of eyes and ears on your vision, offering perspectives you may not have considered.

Yet, there may be a part of you that questions whether you truly deserve such support. This feeling often stems from self-doubt or impostor syndrome—the belief that you're not "good enough" or don't belong in certain spaces. The truth is, you *do* deserve the best support you can get. Everyone, no matter their level of experience or ambition, benefits from a mentor who believes in their potential.

Success requires support, while failure is something we can achieve on our own.

Instead of overwhelming yourself with questions and self-doubt, ask yourself: "Where can I find support? Who can guide me through this challenge?" Seeking mentorship isn't a sign of weakness; it's an investment in your future and a key ingredient to lasting success.

3. Community: The Power of Collective Strength

The third pillar of the Success Triangle is community. Surrounding yourself with like-minded individuals who share your aspirations is incredibly empowering. A supportive community provides motivation during tough times and offers a platform on which to celebrate your successes.

While living in Boston, my friend Caitlin invited me to join a community event called the November Project. This group met every week for early morning fitness exercises. The instructions were simple: show up at the Harvard Stadium Steps at 6 a.m. on Saturday.

Doubts ran through my mind as I woke up early that morning and headed toward the stadium, but once I arrived, I was immediately energized by the sight of hundreds of people who had gathered to climb the steps.

There were all kinds of people—pregnant women, seniors, athletes—each pushing themselves alongside everyone else. I was inspired and had an incredible time participating. The energy was contagious, and people were cheering each other on nonstop. Whenever I felt like giving up, the community's support kept me going. I felt a deep sense of belonging.

I would never have pushed myself to do something like this on my own. This is the power of community—it pushes you to do things you wouldn't attempt by yourself.

In Thriving Coach Academy, our students often express how valuable the community aspect is. As one of our students, Tess, said, "Once I got into the training and was surrounded by other coaches, I realized I was with a group of people who were on the same discovery as I was. I felt really engulfed in the process of showing up fully, playing big, and impacting the lives of others."

Embrace Your Entrepreneurial Potential

If you've ever felt a wave of doubt when considering entrepreneurship, you're not alone. It's common to think, "Oh, here's a new goal...but what about all those other goals I haven't achieved? Will this just be another failure?" It's essential to recognize that these feelings of inadequacy don't stem from a lack of ability or determination.

Instead, they often arise because, like many others, you may not have had all three ingredients of the Success Triangle— frameworks, mentorship, and community—available to you.

When you attempt to tackle a new challenge without the proper support, it's natural to feel overwhelmed. However, understanding that past shortcomings do not define your potential today is crucial. By incorporating the foundational components of the Success Triangle into your entrepreneurial journey, you can create a more robust framework for success.

To guarantee your success as an entrepreneur, answer these three questions:

1. Where can I acquire the knowledge and frameworks?
2. Who can provide me with mentorship and support?
3. How can I surround myself with others who share similar goals?

Entrepreneurship is not about fitting a specific mold. You have the potential to succeed. All you need are the right frameworks, a passionate mentor, and an encouraging community.

You can carve your own path and live on your own terms. The entrepreneur within you is waiting to emerge, so embrace it, nurture it, and watch as you begin to flourish.

CHAPTER 22

The Illusion of Job Security

We've all been sold a lie. That's right. *Everyone* has been sold a lie. From the moment we stepped into school, we were fed a narrative about what success looks like: get a good education, land a stable job, and work your way up the corporate ladder. It's a path drummed into us by parents, teachers, and society at large. But here's the cold, hard truth: depending on someone else for your paycheck is a risky, unreliable, and downright irresponsible way to secure your future.

The myth of job security dates back to the industrial revolution. This was a time when factories boomed and businesses needed a steady workforce to keep production rolling. In response, employers offered attractive wages, benefits, and promises of long-term employment. For decades, this arrangement worked—companies thrived with loyal workers, and employees enjoyed steady pay and job stability.

That sense of security became deeply ingrained in our culture, shaping education systems and career advice across generations. Schools push students toward careers in established industries, and parents—often having experienced an era of lifelong employment—passed down these values. For many years, it seemed like the only path to success.

The truth is, working for someone else is far less secure than it appears. Just look at what happened during the COVID-19 pandemic. Millions of people around the world—perhaps even you or someone close to you—lost their jobs almost overnight as businesses closed, downsized, or collapsed entirely. Entire industries once considered stable crumbled, and livelihoods were uprooted in an instant. The very idea of job security was exposed as an illusion.

And it's not just global crises that threaten traditional employment. Mergers, acquisitions, corporate restructuring, and automation wipe out jobs across every industry. Despite your hard work or loyalty, you could be laid off due to cost-cutting measures, outsourcing, or technology replacing your role. Worse still, internal politics and company profits—factors beyond your control—often dictate promotions and raises.

In a system where your fate is determined by forces outside your control, how secure can your future really be?

Retirement: A Fading Promise

Many people still count on their jobs to secure their retirement. They rely on company-sponsored pension plans, retirement savings accounts, and government-provided benefits to carry them through their golden years. These systems are often considered to be the safety nets that will ensure a comfortable retirement.

However, this faith in external systems is increasingly misplaced. Companies can change their retirement policies whenever it suits them—reducing contributions, altering benefits, or eliminating pension plans altogether. And while many countries offer some form of government-provided retirement benefits, the sustainability of these programs is under strain. Aging populations, shrinking workforces, and the rising cost of living are making it difficult for governments to maintain the levels of support previous generations enjoyed.

In many cases, the money retirees have saved or been promised is no longer enough to cover rising healthcare costs, housing, and day-to-day expenses. Many people who thought they'd be able to retire comfortably are finding themselves forced to continue working well into their later years.

If you're serious about securing your financial future, it's time to rethink your approach to income. Relying on an employer or government system to take care of you is not the answer.

The Most Logical Path to Financial Freedom: Be Your Own Boss

Here's the bottom line: the most responsible way to ensure your financial freedom is to become your own source of income. When you depend on someone else for your paycheck, you're playing a game with stakes you can't afford to lose. But taking control of your financial destiny through entrepreneurship puts you in a position of true power and security.

As your own boss, you dictate how much you earn, how hard you work, and when you grow. The ceiling on your income is determined only by your ambition. There's no waiting for annual reviews, no hoping for a promotion, and no worrying about layoffs or company downsizing. You can build a business that serves your lifestyle, not the other way around.

During the pandemic, while many industries suffered, the coaching industry thrived. As traditional jobs disappeared, people sought guidance, support, and personal growth through professional coaching. The demand for coaches surged, highlighting an essential truth: in uncertain times, people seek leaders who can help them navigate challenges. Coaches became indispensable, proving that entrepreneurship—especially in service-based industries like coaching—offers resilience even when the world around you is unstable.

True Job Security: Uncapped Earning Potential

When you work for yourself, you're no longer tied to a fixed salary. You set your own rates, choose your own clients, and scale your business according to *your* goals—not those of someone else. Unlike a typical job, where your earnings are capped, entrepreneurship offers limitless growth potential.

You can decide to work with a handful of clients, or you can expand, hire a team, and create a thriving enterprise. The choice is yours.

Beyond financial growth, being your own boss gives you personal freedom. You can design your work around your passions, align your career with your values, and enjoy a sense of autonomy that a 9-to-5 job simply can't provide. You're no longer confined by office politics, rigid schedules, or the pressures of corporate life. Instead, you get to chart your own course and prioritize your own well-being.

How Coaching Creates Stability in an Unstable World

The coaching industry is particularly well-suited for individuals seeking both job security and the opportunity to make an impact. In times of change—whether it's personal, professional, or global—people turn to coaches for clarity and direction. As a coach, you become a trusted guide who helps others navigate uncertainty, and in doing so, you create security for yourself.

As bizarre as it sounds, the more chaos there is in the world, the more demand there is for coaches. People need guidance, structure, and a sense of purpose, especially in turbulent times. This means that as a coach, your business has the potential to thrive no matter what the economy is doing.

In the end, the only person you can truly rely on to secure your financial future is you. Becoming your own boss also means you take control of your earnings, your time, and your career trajectory. Instead of leaving your fate in the hands of an employer, a market, or a government system, you create your own opportunities.

There's no question that building a business takes effort and dedication, but the rewards far outweigh the risks. You'll no longer live in fear of layoffs, company restructuring, or pension cuts. Instead, you'll have the freedom to design the life you want—one where your financial future is secure because *you* are the one in control.

CHAPTER 23

Healing Your Relationship With Money

Growing up, my parents constantly fought about money. Their arguments would start small and escalate quickly, sometimes to the point where the shouting got so loud the neighbors would call the police. I'll never forget the nights when the cops came to our home to break up my parents' arguments. Eventually, the fighting reached a breaking point, and they got divorced.

After the divorce, we had to sell the home I grew up in. One minute, I had a sense of endless security, a childhood that felt stable and happy. Then, in what seemed like the blink of an eye, it was all gone. Losing that home was like losing a piece of my identity, a place where I felt safe. As a child, this was devastating.

In the aftermath, I internalized these experiences to mean money was bad. I believed that money was the root cause of my family's conflicts and that it had torn my family apart. Every argument seemed to center around bills, debts, or spending decisions, so to me, it was clear: money was the enemy. I thought money was something dangerous— something to be viewed with fear and suspicion.

I developed a mindset that linked money to conflict, and since conflict was something I wanted to avoid at all costs, I convinced myself that money must be something to avoid as well. If you accumulated money, bad things would happen. If you gave people money, they would take advantage of you. It felt like a constant push and pull. I didn't want to hold onto money because I thought it would bring conflict, but I also feared losing it.

Fast forward to when I first started my coaching business. The conflicting feelings about money were still there, and they showed up in different ways. I didn't want to become the kind of person I associated with wealth—cold, selfish, or manipulative. At the same time, I was terrified of investing money into my business. I had a lingering belief that whatever I put in, I would lose. The memories of my parents' financial struggles haunted me. I thought that just like in my childhood, money could slip away in an instant, and I'd be left with nothing.

I realized if I wanted to succeed in my business and create the life I dreamed of, I needed to change my relationship with money. I felt stuck, caught between my fears and my aspirations. It took deep reflection and time, but I began to shift how I thought about money. I realized money itself wasn't the problem—it was my relationship with it that needed healing.

Money Is a Tool, Not the Enemy

You might relate to some of these feelings, especially if you've grown up witnessing financial struggles or hearing negative beliefs about money. Perhaps you've even asked yourself, "Why should I try to make more money when there are so many people suffering in the world?" It's a valid concern, but the truth is, you can't give what you don't have. The more money you make, the more you can contribute to the causes you care about. When you thrive, you have the capacity to help others thrive too.

Abundance is your birthright. You are here on this planet to flourish. There's nothing noble or kind about undercharging for your services. Undercharging doesn't help anyone else feel more worthy or supported; it simply limits your own ability to give. By denying yourself financial success, you're also denying the greater impact you could have on the world.

Wealth Magnifies Who You Already Are

I've spoken to many people who worry that becoming a successful business owner will cause them to lose their values.

They fear they might lose their soul or become someone they don't recognize as they become more financially successful. Society often feeds us the narrative that wealth and compassion cannot coexist—that rich people must be selfish or exploitative to get where they are. But this couldn't be further from the truth.

The reality is, money is only a magnifier. It doesn't change who you are; it amplifies what's already inside you. If you're a generous, kind, and compassionate person, having more money will increase your capacity to give and serve. The more money you have, the more you can do for the world.

Imagine calling an electrician to fix the wiring in your home. You don't feel guilty paying them, because you recognize the importance of their expertise—and they don't feel guilty getting paid. They solve a problem that improves your quality of life, ensuring your home is safe and functional.

In the same way, as a coach, you're helping people improve their lives, whether it's guiding them through personal challenges or helping them achieve their goals. The money exchanged for that service isn't something to feel guilty about—it's a reflection of the value and transformation you provide.

Another common belief people hold is that wealthy people are inherently evil or opportunistic. This thought is not only unhelpful, it's also untrue. There are good and bad people in every income bracket—there are generous wealthy people and selfish poor people, just as there are kind poor people and greedy wealthy ones. The key is to recognize that wealth isn't what makes someone good or bad—it's their actions and values that matter.

If you believe wealthy people are evil, you will subconsciously sabotage your own chances of creating wealth. Why? Because you don't want to become what you despise. If you hold the belief that money corrupts, you'll resist any opportunity to build wealth, even if it could benefit you and your loved ones. Your mindset will block the very abundance you desire.

On the flip side, wealthy people can be some of the most philanthropic individuals in the world. Take the Giving Pledge, for example—a campaign where some of the world's wealthiest people pledge to give the majority of their wealth to charitable causes. Hundreds of millionaires and billionaires have signed onto this pledge, committing to use their financial success to make the world a better place.

Take a moment and consider these questions:

- How will your success as a coach allow you to give back on a greater scale?
- How will accumulating wealth enable you to create a bigger impact in the world?
- How would building wealth change the lives of your loved ones?

Money allows you to take care of yourself so that you can show up fully for others. It's like the oxygen mask on a plane—you have to put on your own mask before you can help someone else with theirs.

We need more compassionate, heart-centered people to become as wealthy as possible. This is how we raise the consciousness of our planet. If you care about the suffering in the world, then staying broke doesn't help anyone. The more money you have, the more you can donate, invest in meaningful causes, and contribute to the well-being of others.

It's okay to want more money. You can desire wealth and still be a good person. You are allowed to want to help people and make money at the same time. There's no need to choose one over the other—both are possible, and both are necessary.

CHAPTER 24

The Truth About Marketing

For many aspiring coaches, the mere mention of the word "marketing" can elicit a deep sense of dread. It conjures images of awkward sales pitches, intrusive advertisements, and the anxiety of "putting themselves out there." The worry of seeming annoying or insincere can feel overwhelming. While these fears are real, they come from common myths and misunderstandings that can hold back even the most eager coaches.

Many coaches have assumptions about what marketing really means. Let's look at a few:

Assumption #1: Marketing Means Annoying Others.

There's a common belief that effective marketing means bombarding people with messages until they relent and give in. This perspective can make marketing feel like an uphill battle.

Assumption #2: Marketing Means Convincing and Persuading.

Many think marketing focuses on manipulating people into working with you. This view can make anyone feel like a used car salesman—pressure-laden and desperate.

Assumption #3: Marketing Means Using High-Pressure Tactics.

The notion that you need to pressure people into making decisions can be a major turn-off. Think of those infomercials with countdown timers urging you to "act now"—it's enough to make anyone change the channel.

Assumption #4: Marketing Means Being Inauthentic.

There's a fear that marketing demands you to be someone you're not, projecting a false image to attract clients. This can feel like wearing a mask that doesn't fit, leading to a lack of genuine connection.

These assumptions make marketing seem like an unpleasant necessity rather than a valuable and enjoyable aspect of your coaching business. But marketing, when approached correctly, is none of these things.

In the coaching industry, the most effective forms of marketing are rooted in *authenticity, connection*, and a *genuine desire to serve*. Let's break down what marketing actually means and how you can approach it in a way that feels natural and fulfilling.

Attracting Clients vs. Finding Clients

There is a huge difference between *attracting clients* versus *finding them*. Finding clients can feel like constantly chasing people down, pushing your services, or relying on transactional tactics. It's exhausting and often leads to cold responses. You might picture it as sprinting after a bus that is already leaving the station—no matter how fast you run, you may never catch it.

Here's what the Finding Clients Mindset sounds like:

- "How can I generate leads quickly?"
- "What can I do to close the deal?"
- "How can I convince people to hire me?"

In contrast, attracting clients involves creating value and building relationships that naturally draw people to you. When you attract clients, they come to you because they already see the value you provide. This mindset shift is the key to building a sustainable and enjoyable coaching business.

Here's what the Attracting Clients Mindset sounds like:

- "How can I provide value to my audience?"
- "What insights can I share that will resonate with my ideal clients?"
- "How can I build long-term relationships based on trust?"

By focusing on attraction over pursuit, you'll create a coaching business that feels aligned, sustainable, and authentic—allowing clients to naturally gravitate toward you because they see the value you bring.

Marketing Is About Providing Value

At its core, marketing is about *giving value first*. The more you give without attachment, the more you attract. You'll find yourself making more money than you ever imagined, not because you were pushing for it, but because you were genuinely serving and connecting. When people receive something beneficial for free, they often wonder, "If I'm getting so much for free, imagine what I could gain if I *invested* in this person!"

For example, I host a free podcast called *Life Coaching Secrets* with over 200 episodes. This podcast is still active with new episodes shared every month. Each episode aims to provide value without any expectation of return. Ironically, when you detach from the desire to gain clients and focus on genuinely serving, clients often find their way to you.

There are various forms of value you can create: workbooks, templates, videos, journals, podcasts, social media posts, workshops, and webinars. Each piece should aim to deliver a *micro-transformation* for your audience—a small but meaningful shift in their perspective or knowledge that brings them closer to their goals. Over time, these micro-transformations add up, and that's when your clients start pouring in.

Marketing Is About Connecting with People

At the heart of successful marketing lies connection. In a world where people feel more isolated and lonely, connection is craved more than ever before. Invest time in interacting with your network and audience.

Rather than try to constantly grow your following, what if you focused on connecting with your current following? A coach who is deeply connected with a small audience will have more success than a coach who has a larger audience that doesn't feel connected to them.

Reach out to people, start a conversation, respond to comments and messages, ask questions, and listen to their responses. When people feel seen, heard, and understood, they are more likely to trust you and consider working with you. Just as in social situations, where no one enjoys conversing with someone who only talks about themselves, people are drawn to coaches who genuinely want to get to know others.

Marketing Is About Having Fun

Several years ago, I was invited to deliver a short workshop to a group of nearly 100 holistic practitioners in the Bay Area. My mission was to make the largest impact possible in twelve minutes.

As I stepped on stage, I placed my script on a stand and started sharing my presentation. Things were going smoothly for the first few minutes. Then, my notes suddenly slipped off the stand and scattered all over the stage.

My presentation went from polished and professional to chaotic and improvised. At that moment, I realized I had a choice: I could be bothered by the mishap and clean up the mess, or I could just go with the flow and keep the audience engaged.

I decided to see it as an opportunity to have fun and form a deeper connection with the audience. I took one glance at the papers and said, "Buh-bye! I guess that's not happening!" giving a little wave to the pile of papers.

The audience chuckled along with me, and all the tension dissolved. I felt myself relax and shared the rest of my presentation from the heart. Instead of getting it right, I decided to get it real instead.

At the end of my presentation, I briefly mentioned my coaching services, yet I was completely detached from the possibility of enrolling any clients from the presentation. The audience gave a round of applause, and I stepped off the stage. I assumed I hadn't gained any clients from my presentation. But just moments later, an attendee approached me with a warm smile.

"I really enjoyed your presentation," she said. "In fact, I filled out the registration form to hire you!"

Surprised, I asked her, "What inspired you to say yes to my offer?"

She grinned and replied, "It was the moment you dropped your script. Right then, I saw who you truly were—authentic, human, and not afraid to be real. That authenticity sold me."

As I absorbed her words, one of the event coordinators walked up to me, holding a stack of filled-out registration forms.

"These are from other attendees who also decided to hire you," she said, handing me the pile.

Stunned, I flipped through the stack. I had enrolled eight clients that day—all because I embraced the moment, let go of trying to be perfect, and simply connected with the audience from the heart. It was a powerful reminder that sometimes, letting people see the real you is all it takes to make an impact.

The experience taught me a valuable lesson: people connect with who you are, not who you're trying to be. Authenticity has a way of cutting through the noise and leaving a lasting impression. When I let go of perfection and just showed up as myself, I found that others were drawn to that honesty.

Even if your marketing isn't perfect—whether you have typos, stumble over your words, or make mistakes—your genuine energy will resonate more than flawless execution. Authenticity speaks volumes, and your potential clients will appreciate your candidness and relate to your journey.

*In the end, marketing isn't something you **have** to do as a coach; it's something you **get** to do.*

You get the opportunity to share value, connect with people, and have fun. That's all that marketing is. When you shift your focus to the value you are giving others, marketing becomes a joy rather than a chore. Embrace marketing as an exciting part of your coaching journey, and it will feel like an authentic extension of who you already are.

CHAPTER 25

You Have Nothing To Prove

The phone consultation with a potential client was going smoothly—until she asked a question that hit me like a punch in the gut.

"Why should I hire you?"

As her words sank in, my heart began to race and a wave of tension surged through my body. Here I was, desperate to impress and prove my worth, but the reality of the moment felt overwhelming.

I felt the instinctive urge to validate my existence. The weight of her expectations pressed down on me, compelling me to justify my credentials, experience, and unique coaching style. My mind scrambled, ready to recite a laundry list of reasons why I was the best choice.

Before that phone call, I had spent so much of my life trying to prove myself to others. From my family to my teachers, I felt an incessant need to earn their approval. I vividly remember my teenage years when I first realized I was gay. I felt less worthy in a world that seemed to reward conformity. I overcompensated, striving for excellence in academics and extracurricular activities, thinking that if I excelled, I could mask my perceived shortcomings.

I spent years of my life trapped in a cycle of seeking approval, always chasing after the next achievement to feel worthy. I believed I needed to prove my worth through accolades, success, and external validation.

In that moment, I took a deep breath, paused, and a powerful realization settled over me: *I have absolutely nothing to prove.*

I said, "That's a great question. And honestly, it's one I encourage you to consider deeply. This coaching relationship has to feel right for you. Rather than me listing reasons why you should hire me, let's focus on what you need. What is it you're looking for in a coach?"

The entire energy of the conversation shifted. Instead of it being me trying to convince someone to hire me, I simply trusted in my value while inviting her to explore her own intentions and expectations. By the end of the call, she became a five-figure client. And it required me proving nothing at all. I was completely detached from whether or not she would hire me. Instead of leading with Proving Energy, I led with Knowing Energy.

That phone call transformed my approach to marketing my business. I began to understand that marketing is not about proving why people should work with you. Instead, it's about giving value, connecting with others, and inviting them to explore the possibilities you offer.

Proving Energy vs. Knowing Energy

Proving Energy is rooted in the need for external validation. It is driven by a desire to demonstrate worthiness, competence, and success to others. When you operate from Proving Energy, you often feel like you have to *convince* people of your value and justify why you deserve their attention, time, or money.

In business, Proving Energy might manifest in trying too hard to impress clients or customers, pushing them to choose you. It can make you feel anxious and attached to outcomes, fearing that rejection or failure means you aren't good enough. Proving Energy is exhausting. It requires that you're always "on," constantly trying to impress or meet others' expectations. It creates a cycle of over-explaining, overworking, and overthinking.

Knowing Energy, on the other hand, is grounded in self-assurance and inner confidence. You understand that you have nothing to prove because your worth is inherent— it doesn't depend on external approval. Knowing Energy comes from a deep understanding of who you are and what you offer. You're not chasing validation because you already know your value, and you trust that it will be recognized by those who resonate with you.

Knowing Energy is calm and grounded. You're at peace with yourself and can approach situations with ease, without feeling like you have to "perform" or impress others. When someone questions you or doesn't see your value, you don't take it personally because you recognize that their opinion doesn't define your worth. You trust your own judgment and don't need constant affirmation from others to feel successful.

In business, Knowing Energy translates into offering your services with confidence, knowing that you are enough as you are. Instead of trying to convince others to work with you, you invite them to see the value in what you provide. You detach from the outcome and trust that the right clients will come. This creates a relaxed, magnetic energy that naturally attracts those who align with your message.

Imagine going into a networking event with Proving Energy. You might over-prepare, creating a list of all your achievements, awards, and successes to make sure everyone sees you as the best option. You feel anxious throughout the event, and if they question your methods or price, you feel defensive and eager to justify yourself.

Now imagine approaching the networking event with Knowing Energy. You walk calmly and confidently, trusting that your worth is non-negotiable. You're more focused on getting to know people and how you can help them, rather than trying to impress them. If they question your methods or price, you remain unbothered, explaining your approach without the need to prove why you're worth it. If they choose not to work with you, you trust that it's simply not the right fit, and you remain open to other opportunities.

When you feel yourself slipping into Proving Energy, pause and remind yourself that your role isn't to convince or prove your value to potential clients—it's to offer genuine value and connect with those who resonate with your approach. Instead, shift your focus back to how you can help your ideal clients. Ask yourself, "How can I serve and connect?" rather than "How can I prove myself?"

Ground yourself in the belief that the right clients will be drawn to you for who you are, not because of how much you "prove" your worth. By focusing on giving value and trusting in your expertise, you can market with authenticity and ease, allowing potential clients to feel a connection and choose to work with you from a place of trust, not persuasion.

Proving Energy	Knowing Energy
Fear-based. Fear of not being enough drives you to prove yourself.	**Trust-based.** Inner knowing that you are enough without needing external validation.
Focused on external validation. Your worth is tied to others' opinions, approval, and recognition.	**Focused on internal validation.** Your worth comes from within, and you trust in your value.
Defensive and reactive. You feel the need to justify your abilities and defend yourself when questioned.	**Calm and receptive.** You remain grounded and confident, regardless of others' opinions or judgments.
Scarcity mindset. You feel like there isn't enough success or opportunity to go around, leading to competition and comparison.	**Abundance mindset.** You believe that there's enough for everyone, and you're open to opportunities and collaboration.
Anxious and attached to outcomes. You're constantly worried about results and how others perceive you.	**Detached from outcomes.** You trust that the right people and opportunities will be drawn to you without forcing anything.

Your Worth Is Non-Negotiable

Every human is born with intrinsic worthiness. We are worthy because we exist, not because of what we accomplish or how others perceive us. We don't need to earn this worth—it's an unchangeable part of who we are. Our worth as individuals is not tied to achievements, status, or others' perceptions; it's something you possess simply by being alive.

When you operate from a place of needing to prove yourself, you give away your power. You allow others to dictate your worth based on their standards, expectations, and judgments. On the other hand, when you recognize that you have nothing to prove, you take back that power and root your self-esteem in your values, integrity, and sense of purpose.

Letting go of the need to prove yourself allows you to focus on being your true self. Ironically, this authenticity builds trust far more effectively than any attempt to impress others. When you stop seeking validation, you create an atmosphere of authenticity that resonates with others. Clients are drawn to genuine connections; they can sense when someone is being real. By showing up as your true self, you naturally attract the right clients who resonate with your message and values.

Your authenticity becomes your magnet, drawing opportunities and clients toward you. You no longer chase after success; it comes to you because you're being who you were meant to be. Embracing your inherent worth doesn't just liberate you; it opens the door to abundance, fulfillment, and genuine connection in your coaching career.

Remember: you have nothing to prove.

CHAPTER 26

One on One vs. Group Coaching

As my coaching business gained momentum, I reached a point where I was coaching eight people a day. At first, I thought I had made it. I was earning great money and making a real impact in my clients' lives. But there was a problem—time. I had created financial success, but I lacked the time freedom that I truly craved. Every day was filled with back-to-back sessions, and I barely had time to breathe, let alone enjoy the success I had worked so hard to achieve.

One day, exhausted from a long day of one-on-one coaching, I asked myself, "What if I could coach multiple clients at once by offering group coaching?" It was a lightbulb moment. Not only could I shrink the number of hours I worked, but I could also take on more clients, increase my impact, and ultimately make more money.

That's exactly what I did. I transitioned most of my clients into group coaching programs, and the impact was incredible—not just for me, but for my clients too. Not only did I free up 80 percent of my time, but I was able to take on more clients and generate more revenue without sacrificing quality.

The Power of Group Coaching

Group coaching creates a new kind of experience for clients. Bringing people together allows them to gain fresh insights, connect with others on similar journeys, and feel supported. Clients often find that sharing the process with others adds a level of motivation and connection that makes the journey even more powerful. Here are the five main benefits of group coaching:

1. **Scalability**. One of the best ways to scale your coaching business is by offering group coaching. Unlike one-on-one coaching, group coaching allows you to work with multiple clients at once, which instantly frees up more time in your schedule.

2. **Community.** Group coaching creates a strong sense of community. Your clients aren't just learning from you; they're connecting with each other, sharing similar challenges, and working toward common goals. This creates camaraderie, a key ingredient in any successful coaching program. Many people feel isolated when facing personal challenges, thinking they are the only ones going through it. But in a group, clients realize they're not alone. Knowing that others are on the same journey gives them the courage to open up, seek support, and stick with the process.

3. **Shared Experience.** Additionally, the shared experience of group coaching fosters deeper learning. Your clients will not only learn from your expertise but also gain valuable insights from the experiences and perspectives of their peers. When clients share their wins, challenges, and personal breakthroughs, everyone benefits. This amplifies the learning process in ways that one-on-one coaching simply can't match.

4. **Accessibility.** Another significant advantage of group coaching is that it's more accessible. If a potential client is hesitant to invest in high-ticket one-on-one coaching, group coaching provides a more affordable entry point for these clients, allowing them to experience the value of your coaching at a lower cost before deciding to invest in your premium services. For instance, a group coaching program priced at $497 can serve as an introduction to your coaching. Later, you can offer a $5,000 one-on-one program to those who are ready for a more personalized experience.

5. **Accountability.** Group coaching also fosters peer accountability. When clients collaborate and support each other outside of scheduled sessions, it reinforces their commitment to their goals. At Thriving Coach Academy, we organize our coaches into peer groups during their training. These groups meet regularly to practice coaching techniques, discuss their progress, and hold each other accountable. This peer support structure not only boosts results but also deepens connections between clients.

Some coaches worry clients won't get enough individual attention in a group setting, but that's rarely the case. Clients can learn just as much from witnessing someone else's coaching session as they would from being in the "hot seat" themselves. Plus, not everyone in the group will want to be coached during every session, but they will still benefit by listening and relating to others' experiences. This collective learning experience often deepens their understanding and accelerates their progress.

Two Models for Pricing Group Coaching

When it comes to pricing your group coaching program, you have two main options: the One-And-Done Model and the Subscription Model.

In the One-And-Done Model, clients pay a single fee upfront to join the program, which has set start and end dates. You could charge $2,000 for a three-month group coaching program and offer enrollment during specific "launch" periods throughout the year. When clients finish the program, they can choose to finish their coaching journey or join a waitlist for the next round.

In the Subscription Model, clients pay a recurring fee to stay in your program as long as they want. For example, you could charge $500 per month with the option to cancel anytime. To incentivize long-term commitments, you could offer a discounted rate for clients who commit to a full year, such as $5,000 annually instead of $6,000. This model provides you with a steady stream of recurring revenue and encourages ongoing engagement from your clients.

Suppose you offer a group coaching program with a one-hour session each week, charging $1,000 per client. With 20 clients attending the same weekly session, you would earn $20,000 a month while working only one hour per week with the group. As your client base grows, you could also bring on additional coaches to lead other group sessions, giving you even greater flexibility and freedom.

Balancing the Benefits of One-on-One Coaching

While group coaching has many advantages, one-on-one coaching still holds a special place in the coaching world. Personalized, individual attention can be incredibly impactful, especially when clients are dealing with deeply personal or complex challenges. In one-on-one coaching, you can tailor every session to a client's unique needs, providing more customized feedback and support.

One-on-one coaching also allows for more intimate and focused conversations. This deep connection helps build trust and rapport, which are essential for guiding clients through their most challenging obstacles. The more personalized the experience, the deeper the transformation can be.

However, the downside of one-on-one coaching is that it limits your ability to scale your business. There are only so many hours in the day, and I recommend you have no more than three one-on-one clients in a day. While one-on-one coaching can command higher prices, it may not be sustainable in the long run if you're looking for more freedom in your life.

Both models have their advantages, and you can choose the one that best fits your business goals and the needs of your clients. The key is to create a structure that supports both you and your clients, offering them tremendous value while giving you the freedom to enjoy the life you're building.

CHAPTER 27

Having the Confidence to Charge

D
o you cringe at the thought of selling your services? Are you worried you'll come off as pushy, aggressive or salesy? If so, you're not alone. In today's world, we are constantly being sold something through ads, emails and social media. For many, this creates a negative relationship

with being sold to. The last thing you want is to feel like a walking sales pitch everyone's trying to avoid.

While we might not always welcome ads, think about the products or services that have improved your quality of life. Maybe it's a high-quality mattress that has changed how you sleep, a kitchen appliance that has elevated cooking at home, or a course that has transformed your life. Without some form of promotion, you may never have discovered them, and your life would be missing the value they brought.

Now imagine being the person who offers that kind of value and transformation to others. When they think about the breakthroughs they've achieved because of your coaching, they'll see it as one of the best decisions they ever made. Picture the day when a client looks back on their journey with you and says, "I'm so glad you offered your services—it transformed my entire life."

Selling is *not* about manipulation, forcing, or convincing. It's simply an invitation—a way to offer people something that could benefit them. It's about presenting an opportunity and letting them decide if it's the right fit for their needs and goals. By selling, you're empowering them to make a choice, not pressuring them into one.

Selling doesn't have to be uncomfortable. In fact, when done with the right mindset, it can feel like a natural part of your work. Here are the most common concerns coaches have about charging for their services—and how to overcome them so you can sell with confidence and dignity.

Concern 1:
"I'm afraid people will turn down my coaching."

One of the biggest fears coaches have is that of rejection. When someone says "no," it's easy to personalize it, but rejection is not about you. Often, a "no" means you've been spared from something that wasn't meant for you.

Have you ever had an experience where you thought someone you were dating was right for you, only to later realize you dodged a bullet? It's the same in your coaching business. If someone doesn't want to work with you, it opens the door for an ideal client who does.

Rejection can actually be a form of protection. When you resist the fear of rejection, you create space for clients who are a perfect fit. When you allow desperation to seep into your business, it distorts everything. I've been there—I took on clients who weren't a good fit, and it drained my energy. The effort I could've put into attracting ideal clients was wasted on ones who weren't aligned with my values or vision.

When a client says "no," take it as a sign. They weren't meant to be in your coaching space, and their departure makes room for a better opportunity.

Rejection is freeing when you embrace it. Instead of resisting the "no," thank it. It's a step toward the "yes" that's waiting for you right around the corner.

Concern 2:
"Charging feels like it cheapens what I offer. I'm used to helping people for free, and now it feels weird to charge."

Many coaches feel conflicted when they start charging for their services, especially if they've spent years offering help for free. It might feel unnatural to ask for money for something that comes easily to you. But consider this: when you see a Lamborghini offered at 80 percent off, what's your first thought?

That's right.

"What's wrong with it?"

When we offer our services at low prices or for free, we can unintentionally diminish the perceived value. Charging for your services isn't just about the money—it's about the commitment it inspires in your clients. People who pay, pay attention. When they invest in your coaching, they're more likely to take it seriously and invest in themselves.

I used to give away a lot of coaching sessions for free, and eventually noticed people rarely made meaningful changes with no investment on their part. But when I started charging for my sessions, people showed up more fully. Charging enhances the experience, not cheapens it.

One of my students worked at a nonprofit and struggled with the idea of being paid well for her coaching. She felt that because she was doing valuable work, she didn't need to be compensated much. But that belief was keeping her stuck. We worked through this mindset, and she realized that the idea that she shouldn't charge for her coaching was not actually true—it just allowed her to justify the years of underpayment and undervaluation.

She then realized that by charging what she was truly worth, she could provide even greater value to her clients and herself. This shift allowed her to embrace the idea that receiving fair compensation wasn't selfish—it was a way to elevate her work and create a more sustainable impact. By charging more, she could actually provide a better experience for her clients and herself. What if charging is not bad, but what's bad is how you were conditioned to view money, success, and your own value?

Concern 3:
"I'm putting people in a worse place by charging."

It's normal to feel like you're adding more stress to someone's life when you ask them to invest in coaching, especially if they're already dealing with financial burdens. When someone hires you, they may experience short-term discomfort that sometimes comes with spending money, but the long-term value far outweighs the initial cost.

On the flip side, if someone doesn't invest in themselves through your coaching, they're choosing the short-term comfort of not doing anything over long-term growth. The problem they're facing doesn't disappear; it likely gets worse. So by charging for your services, you're actually helping people move out of their comfort zones and into a space of real transformation.

The short-term discomfort spending money on coaching is nothing compared to the long-term positive impact they will receive from coaching. By charging, you're inviting your clients to experience a deeper commitment to their own growth, which puts them in a better place in the long run.

Concern 4:
"I shouldn't charge for something that comes naturally to me."

This is a belief many coaches have—"If I'm naturally good at something, I shouldn't charge because it doesn't feel like work." Just because something comes easily to you doesn't mean it's any less valuable. The world is full of people who struggle with the very things that come naturally to you. Your gift is your strength, and charging for it allows you to serve more people with that gift.

Moreover, when you charge for something that feels natural, you're allowing yourself to step fully into your purpose. You're modeling for your clients what it looks like to value your own worth. When you value your work, they will too. Charging is not about exploiting your gift—it's about honoring it.

Having the confidence to charge is essential for your growth as a coach. It requires a mindset shift and an openness to seeing the value you provide in a new light. Charging for your services doesn't cheapen what you offer—it elevates it. Rejection isn't something to fear, but something to embrace as it clears the path for your ideal clients. You have unique abilities that deserve recognition, and charging for your services enhances their value rather than diminishes it.

The next time you feel hesitant to charge or worry about putting someone in a difficult position, remind yourself: your work has the potential to make a profound difference in their lives. Trust in your worth, stand confidently in your rates, and remember that you are doing a service by encouraging growth and commitment in those you work with.

When you charge, you're not just inviting clients to invest in you; you're inviting them to invest in themselves. You're giving them the opportunity to experience real transformation, and that's worth every penny. The next time you feel hesitant about charging for your coaching, remind yourself: you're worth it, and so are they.

By now, we've covered how to have a winning mindset when launching your coaching business. In the next section, we'll dive into mastering client attraction. You'll learn how to draw clients to you naturally and make the impact you're here to make. From finding the best places to connect with clients to understanding the psychology of premium clients, you'll gain the insights needed to grow your business with intention and purpose.

TOP 10 INSIGHTS

1. Entrepreneurship isn't about luck or personality—it's about having the right frameworks, mentorship, and community.

2. The most logical path to financial freedom and job security is to be your own boss.

3. As an entrepreneur, you can design a career that aligns with your passions and values while giving you a sense of autonomy that a 9-to-5 job simply can't provide.

4. If you're a generous, kind, and compassionate person, having more money will increase your capacity to give and serve.

5. The most effective marketing is rooted in authenticity, connection, and a genuine desire to serve others.

6. The right clients will be drawn to you for who you are, not because of how much you "prove" your worth.

7. Group coaching offers greater flexibility and accessibility, while one-on-one coaching allows for more personalized feedback and support.

8. When a potential client says a "no", it means you've been spared from something that wasn't meant for you.

9. Your coaching services are an investment clients will look back on with gratitude for its life-changing impact.

10. Charging for your services isn't just about the money—it's about the commitment it inspires in your clients.

SECTION V

Mastering Client Attraction

"Several years ago, I started thinking about my next chapter. I've been in the corporate world, but I didn't want to stay there for the rest of my life. I was drawn to pursue a career in coaching. There are people around me who say, 'Can't you just learn coaching from reading books and watching YouTube videos?' When I estimated how long it would take to do it on my own, I realized the Academy can teach me a proven way to be successful. It would save me time so I don't have to do a lot of trial and error. I was surprised by the depth of what I learned and how simple TCA made everything. Within about six months of enrolling, I quit my full-time job and I'm 100 percent focused on my coaching business. Because of all the support I got from TCA, I feel more confident than the other times I made career changes. I feel like I have all the right information and support. If there are people who are serious about coaching and considering Thriving Coaching Academy, trust the process. It works."

- HOJEONG K.

CHAPTER 28

Your Clients Are Waiting For You

It was a particularly hot summer morning in Seattle, the kind that makes you question every life choice that brought you to a city known for its rain. I was on a mission to find new activities to meet people and get in better shape, preferably at the same time.

After a quick online search for local events, my scrolling came to a screeching halt: "Nude Yoga." Intrigued and slightly horrified, I clicked on the link. Was it really what it sounded like? Yes, it absolutely was. An outdoor yoga session was being held at a clothing-optional beach, just a 30-minute bus ride away.

After a heated internal debate, fueled by equal parts curiosity and insanity, I decided to attend. The bus ride felt like it took an eternity, my mind racing with visions of what awaited me. Arriving at the beach, I noticed a few sunbathers in all their bare-skinned glory, fully embracing the clothing-optional vibe of the place. But then I spotted a group nearby, gathering for yoga.

The instructor, still clothed, stood alongside a few other attendees who were also dressed, appearing just as hesitant as I felt. I approached, clutching my mat with a mix of apprehension and excitement. The instructor greeted us warmly and asked if anyone had injuries or physical conditions to be aware of. We all shook our heads, the nervous silence palpable.

Then, with a confident, "Okay, let's begin," he took the first plunge—stripping down to his birthday suit. The rest of us exchanged a few nervous glances before following suit, each of us shedding our clothes one by one.

In those first moments, I felt completely exposed, trying not to glance at others while simultaneously worrying they'd be looking at me. But as we settled into the practice, the initial awkwardness melted away, and I became just another participant in this unusual but oddly freeing experience.

We twisted and stretched into various poses, one of which was the unforgettable Happy Baby Pose. Picture this: lying on your back, legs in the air, grabbing your feet, and rocking back and forth like a blissful infant. All without any clothing on. Yep, it was quite the sight.

When the session ended, the instructor left, and the other attendees began to drift away. Still naked, I looked around and caught the eye of a man in his fifties with a big smile, blue eyes, and gray hair, also still completely unclothed. He walked over, introduced himself, and we struck up a conversation. As it turned out, this was his first time attending nude yoga too, and we shared a laugh about the unexpected sense of freedom the experience had brought us.

He worked in healthcare insurance and asked what I did. I hesitated, feeling unsure if it was appropriate to bring up my work, especially given that we were both still naked. But after a brief pause, I decided to share. "I'm a life coach," I said. "I offer various transformational workshops and events in the city."

He was intrigued and asked to stay in touch, sharing that he had recently lost the love of his life to cancer and wasn't ready to open his heart again but still wanted to be kept in the loop about my events. I took his card, and we said our goodbyes.

When I got home, I added his email to my mailing list. Hosting workshops every couple of weeks was my main way of marketing my coaching services. Several months later, I was wrapping up a workshop with about twenty attendees when one person lingered behind. This was typical, as some people often stayed to ask questions.

"Do you remember me?" he asked. The attendee looked familiar, but I couldn't place him.

"I know we met somewhere, but please remind me!" I said.

"We met at a nude yoga session over the summer."

"Of course! I remember you!" I had trouble recognizing him with clothes on, since we had met in the nude. "What did you think of the workshop tonight?"

"I want to thank you for adding me to your mailing list and keeping me in touch. When we met, I was not in the space where I was ready to move forward. But now I am."

Long story short, this man ended up paying me $15,000 for one-on-one coaching. We worked together to address the limiting rules he had about his worth, finding love later in life, and loving again after losing a loved one. He had rules like, "I can't find love again because it would betray my late partner," and, "I'm too old to start over."

Through our sessions, he found the courage to open his heart again and fell in love with a wonderful man. They ended up getting married.

Life coaching isn't just about setting goals or breaking bad habits; it's about transforming every layer of a person's life—helping them rewrite their rules, open their hearts, and realize that even in their most vulnerable moments, a richer, more fulfilling future awaits.

The moral of the story is simple: clients are everywhere, and they're often in the most unexpected places. Growing a business is a lot like planting a garden. You can't expect the seeds to bloom overnight. Many of my clients were people I met in person or who found me online. They didn't always hire me immediately, but they eventually did.

Your clients are already waiting for you. Some of them might not be ready to hire you right now, but that doesn't mean they won't in the future. Just like the man I met at the yoga class, people may need time to reach a point where they feel ready to invest in themselves through coaching. And when they are, they'll think of you—because you've stayed present in their lives, offering value without attachment to the outcome.

Your Essence Is Your Superpower

Every person has their own *essence*, a combination of their story, the energy or vibe they give off, and their unique gifts. Your essence is like your fingerprint—completely one-of-a-kind. No one can replicate it, and that's what makes it so valuable.

Your essence matters because it's the very thing that naturally attracts the people who are meant to work with you. It's not about having the perfect marketing plan, saying all the right things, or fitting into some predetermined mold of what a coach should be. It's about showing up as *you*. Your story, your energy, and the way you offer your gifts to the world are exactly what someone out there is looking for.

Think about it—there are countless coaches, speakers, and mentors out there. But no one else can bring *your* unique combination of life experiences, insights, and personality to the table. That's why your essence is so powerful. It will draw people to you who resonate with *who you are*, not just what you do.

You Don't Need to Change—Just Show Up

The best part? You don't have to change a thing about yourself. You don't need to become someone else to be successful or to attract clients. The key is to simply put yourself out there, let people see you, and trust that the right people will be drawn to your essence.

There are people who are waiting to experience *you* right now. They are out there, looking for exactly what you have to offer, even if they don't know it yet. And when they encounter your essence—whether through your content, your presence at an event, or even a chance meeting—they'll feel that pull. They'll sense that you're the person who can help them, not because of any external factors but because of who you are at your core.

Your essence will do the work of attracting the right clients to you. All you need to do is show up and trust in that power.

So take heart, and know that your clients are already out there, waiting to meet you—just as you are out there, waiting to meet them. As long as you stay persistent and keep adding value to others, everything will come back tenfold in the form of paying clients. And sometimes, those clients might just come from a memorable day of nude yoga on the beach.

CHAPTER 29

The Best (and Worst) Ways To Attract Clients

I n my first year as a coach, I had no idea how to attract clients. In a moment of desperation, I printed out flyers and taped them on bulletin boards and telephone poles around a local college campus. I was sure my phone would be ringing off the hook in no time.

But guess what? Not a single person reached out. I didn't understand the difference between finding clients and attracting clients, and I was making all the wrong moves.

Since then, I've learned that attracting clients is much simpler than I thought, and it doesn't require wasting time on strategies that don't work. Below, I'll break down the top five best ways to attract clients—and the five worst ways, which you should avoid.

The Five Best Ways to Attract Clients
(in no particular order)

1.   Networking

When many people think of "networking," they envision formal events filled with business cards and scripted conversations. However, networking is much more about genuine connections and building relationships wherever you are. It can happen in everyday situations—at coffee shops, community events, or even while running errands.

Stay open to opportunities and introduce yourself as a coach whenever you meet someone new. You may be surprised by how often individuals are looking for a coach or know someone who could benefit from your services. The key is to be approachable and authentic, allowing conversations to flow naturally. By fostering these organic interactions, you create an environment where potential clients feel comfortable seeking your guidance.

2.   Speaking Engagements and Live Events

Public speaking is a powerful way to showcase your expertise while delivering value to your audience. You can host your own webinars or workshops, or speak at various events to connect with potential clients. Whether online or in person, live events help build trust and allow attendees to experience your personality and energy firsthand.

When organizing your own events, you have the flexibility to choose the size and duration that align with your preferences. For instance, as an introvert, I found that hosting intimate gatherings with no more than twelve participants worked best for me.

At the end of each event, invite attendees to schedule a consultation, giving them the opportunity to explore working with you. In fact, for several years, I generated a six-figure annual income solely by hosting a few live events each year.

3. Social Media

Social media is an effective way to build relationships and provide value over time. Rather than being on every platform, choose one platform and focus on sharing insights, stories, and content that resonates with your audience. Don't be discouraged by "vanity metrics" such as your number of likes and comments. Do you press "like" on every post you get value from online?

With social media, most of your clients will be silently admiring your content. On social media, consistency is key. By showing up regularly, you build a presence that attracts clients naturally.

4. Podcasting

Podcasts are a great platform to share your expertise and attract clients. You can either start your own podcast or be a guest on someone else's show. This allows you to reach a broader audience, build trust, and establish authority in your niche.

Podcasting lets you provide valuable insights while showcasing your personality and coaching style. It also gives listeners a chance to get to know you over time. Collaborating with other hosts can expand your reach and introduce you to new audiences who may become your future clients.

5. Referrals

Referrals are one of the most reliable ways to attract new clients. Many coaches assume that satisfied clients will naturally refer others, but this is often not the case. It's essential to actively ask for referrals from your current and past clients. Your current network is low-hanging fruit; people you already know likely have connections who would benefit from your services.

This approach can help you enroll your first few clients and gain initial momentum. Additionally, create a "Dream Fifteen" list of individuals, such as micro-influencers or thought leaders in your niche, who connect with your ideal clients. Engaging with them can open doors to new referral opportunities.

Myth: You Have to Do All the Strategies

One common myth that many new coaches believe is that they must utilize every available strategy to attract clients. In reality, you don't have to implement every strategy out there. Instead, you can focus on what truly matters: dialing in on *one* effective approach.

Embrace the **One-One-One Principle**: one niche, one marketing strategy, one million. Concentrate your efforts on one niche and one marketing strategy until you hit your first million. Then, you can expand to more marketing channels if you desire.

This method not only prevents burnout but also helps you build a strong foundation for your coaching business. You'll find this approach makes it easier to attract clients and brings more clarity to your coaching journey, helping you feel more confident and fulfilled in your work.

Five Worst Ways to Find Clients
(also in no particular order)

1. Business Cards

Handing out business cards at random events is a passive approach that rarely works. Most cards get tossed or forgotten, leaving you with no way to follow up or build a connection. It's impersonal and doesn't engage people in a meaningful way. Instead, focus on collecting contact information so you can initiate follow-up conversations. This allows for deeper engagement and the potential for nurturing those connections into client relationships.

2. Paid Ads

Paid ads can be effective, but they're not the best starting point for new coaches. To really benefit from ads, you should be earning at least $30k per month, as they can be costly and take time to yield results. You need to be prepared to spend thousands each month, knowing some ads will work while others won't.

It's crucial to first establish a solid organic marketing strategy and a compelling offer using the five methods mentioned above, ensuring you're financially secure before investing heavily in advertising.

3. Static Website

Many coaches mistakenly believe that simply launching a basic website with their bio, logo, and coaching rates will attract clients. Unfortunately, that's not the case. Instead, create a dynamic site that offers a valuable resource to visitors. This could be a free eBook, checklist, or webinar that requires them to submit their email address through an opt-in form to access it.

This strategy not only provides value but also allows you to start building a relationship with potential clients. By engaging visitors in this way, you reduce the chance of them leaving your site after just one visit, turning your website into a powerful tool for client attraction.

4. Cold Calling

Cold calling is one of the most dreaded and ineffective ways to find clients. Most people are instantly put off by unsolicited calls, perceiving them as intrusions into their day. Rather than engaging in meaningful conversations, recipients often feel pressured and annoyed, making them unlikely to consider your services seriously.

Cold calls come across as pushy and transactional, lacking the personal touch that builds rapport and trust. Additionally, they disrupt the recipient's routine, creating a negative impression of both you and your business. In a world where people crave authentic connections, cold calls often leave potential clients feeling frustrated and uninterested.

5. Begging Friends and Family

You do *not* have to beg family and friends to hire you, so take a deep breath! While asking them for referrals can be helpful, directly seeking their business often leads to awkwardness and discomfort. Relying on friends and family to be your clients can strain relationships and rarely results in sustainable growth. Instead, focus on attracting clients who genuinely value your services. Leave Aunt Joan and Uncle Joe alone—unless you want them to start questioning your career choices over Thanksgiving dinner.

Attracting clients doesn't have to be complicated or feel uncomfortable. The best approach is simple: show up as yourself, focus on building real connections, and keep offering value. Trust that the right clients—those who resonate with you and need what you offer—will come your way. When you stick to what feels natural and true, you'll find that growing your client base becomes both rewarding and sustainable.

CHAPTER 30

The Psychology of Premium Clients

I used to have a twenty-dollar pair of headphones. I didn't take care of these headphones and often shoved them in my pocket when I wasn't using them. After a few months, they'd stop working, and I'd go buy the same cheap pair, knowing they were going to break again.

All the while, I thought I was saving money by opting for the cheaper option, but over time, I realized I was actually spending more. Not just money—but time and frustration. Finally, after a lot of internal resistance, I decided to invest $200 in a high-quality pair of headphones. Part of me couldn't believe I was spending so much money on a pair of headphones.

However, the moment I put on the new headphones, the difference was night and day. The sound quality was so clear and crisp.

Instead of thinking I was ridiculous for buying the expensive headphones, I instead thought how ridiculous it was that I had tolerated cheap headphones for so long! With these new headphones, I felt a sense of responsibility. I thought, "I paid so much, I better take care of them." I still use those same headphones today, many years later.

After this experience, I began to change my buying habits. I started prioritizing value over cost. I actively sought out services and products of higher quality instead of trying to save a few dollars here and there. This shift in mindset enhanced my entire life for the better. I found that investing in premium options led to better experiences, deeper satisfaction, and ultimately, more fulfillment in both my personal and professional pursuits.

When you invest more in something, you value it more, take better care of it, and enjoy a higher quality of life as a result. The same principle applies to coaching: clients who invest in a premium service tend to be more committed, engaged, and open to real transformation. By shifting from a Basic Coaching Business model to a Premium Coaching Business model, you invite clients into a deeper, more impactful experience that fosters lasting change.

The Basic Business Model

Many coaches start with what seems like the most straightforward approach: charge by the hour, keep prices low, and hope to attract as many clients as possible. But this Basic Business Model comes with serious limitations:

1. **You Attract Less Committed Clients**. Low prices bring in clients who aren't fully invested in their own growth. They're looking for a quick fix, not a real transformation. When clients aren't committed, they don't show up fully, and as a coach, that means you're putting in more effort than they are. This leads to frustration, mediocre results, and often clients dropping off halfway through their journey.

2. **Your Income Is Unstable**. With the basic model, you're constantly hustling for your next session, hoping that clients will rebook. This makes your income unpredictable, leaving you in a constant state of stress. You're always chasing the next client just to stay afloat. This isn't sustainable for the long term.

3. **No Freedom**. When you have cheap coaching rates, the only way to earn more is to work more. You will have to manage a full schedule of clients everyday with little time outside of your business. This approach drains your energy and eliminates any possibility for freedom. When you're charging low fees, you're stuck in this grind with little room to scale.

Many coaches assume that if their services are cheaper, they'll sell more easily. This is a myth. Cheaper offers actually come with a higher refund rate. When I first started out, I sold cheap coaching programs, and had a 10 percent refund rate.

But once I raised my rates and sold high-ticket programs, that refund rate became practically zero.

Why? Because people who invest more value the experience more. You don't see people walking into Hermès, Rolex, or Rolls Royce asking for refunds. When someone is willing to invest in a high-ticket offer, they're already committed.

The Premium Business Model

The good news is you don't have to be trapped in a Basic Business Model. There is a solution, and it's called the Premium Business Model. This is designed for coaches who want to make a high impact and income. In this business model, you sell a high-ticket program (a program that you sell for $5,000 and up) or a group coaching program (which allows you to coach multiple people in a group setting). Both approaches allow you to scale your business to unlimited earning potential.

Scaling gives you the freedom and time to enjoy your life. For example, you could have just one to three client sessions per day, leaving the rest of your time free. Alternatively, you could have a single one-hour group session where you support a handful of clients, again freeing up a significant amount of your time. This flexibility means you can focus on delivering quality coaching without feeling overwhelmed.

When you have a Premium Business Model, you attract clients who are serious about making a change. These clients aren't just dabbling; they're all in. They've made a significant financial commitment, which means they show up fully, ready to do the work. This is the key to creating powerful transformations—both for them and for you as a coach.

By working with fewer, higher-paying clients, you can focus more deeply on each one, giving them the best possible experience. This leads to better outcomes and a more rewarding coaching practice for you. Plus, when you're not hustling for clients all the time, you avoid any risk of burnout. The Premium Business Model gives you the freedom to work with fewer clients while still earning more.

The Three Types of Buyers

The question you are likely having right now is, "Are there people out there who will really invest that much for coaching?" The answer is yes, and I will explain why. When it comes to any purchasing decision in life, there are three categories of buyers: Freeples, Cheeples, and Preeples.

Freeples are people who want everything for free. You can offer them something for a dollar and they'd say, "Why isn't it free?" If you tell a Freeple what you charge as a coach, they will question it. It doesn't mean you shouldn't be charging for coaching. It just means that you're talking to a Freeple.

Then we have the **Cheaples**. These are people who are looking to spend, but want everything for a low price. They want the best discount, and they will likely try to negotiate the price down. They try to minimize the cost as much as they can, even if it means losing out on the value of the product or service.

Last, there are **Preeples**. They are people who *want* to pay a premium. They are not thinking, "How much does this cost?" They think, "What will give me the most value?" When they buy things, they focus on what they are gaining, not what they are losing. Preeples have a higher quality of life because they get the results they want faster. They buy things that may be costly upfront, but save them much more time, money, and effort in the long run.

To be clear, this is not about selling your coaching solely to ultra-wealthy people. We all have areas of our lives that we demonstrate Preeple behavior. For example, it could be fashion, technology, furniture, or food. There is likely an area or two in your life where you prioritize value over cost.

Some people put a high value on their own personal growth and education. These are the people who want high-end coaching services. They will deliberately avoid cheaper options because they desire something substantial.

There are countless premium coaching clients out there, yet so few coaches are actively marketing to them. By learning to create a high-ticket offer and effectively market it to the Premium Buyer, you will be tapping into this ocean of untapped potential.

With this in mind, you don't have to charge a high ticket right out the gate. For my first couple of clients, I didn't charge them anything at all, with the condition that if they got value, they would provide me with a testimonial. This allowed me to gain a lot of confidence when I began working with my clients because I got to see how well the coaching process worked.

After seeing the difference coaching made in their lives, I believed more deeply in myself as a coach. For my first few paying clients, I charged about $100 per client. For my next few clients, I charged $250 per client. Before I knew it, I was charging $5,000 to $10,000 per client. These were clients who were grateful and excited to work together. As your confidence grows, allow your coaching rates to grow as well.

If you aspire to live a life of freedom and live on your own terms, embracing a Premium Business Model is essential.

By understanding the value you provide and attracting those who are willing to invest in their growth, you position yourself for financial success and personal fulfillment. A premium model not only allows you to make a significant impact on your clients' lives, but also grants you the flexibility and independence you desire.

Don't settle for a Basic Business Model that limits your potential—choose to elevate your coaching business and unlock the freedom that comes with it. When you are the cheapest coach, no one expects you to be the best. When you are the best coach, no one expects you to be the cheapest.

CHAPTER 31

How To Choose A Niche

A re there too many life coaches out there?

The truth is both yes and no. Yes, there are many life coaches, but no, there is not an oversaturation of highly trained and specialized coaches. The key difference lies in specialization. A coach who is highly trained in a specific area, a *niche*, stands out from the generalist crowd.

Aspects of the industry might be oversaturated, but specialized coaches that have a clear market or problem they focus on are very valuable. Think about it like this: if you had a heart problem, would you go to a general doctor or a cardiologist? Most likely, you'd choose the cardiologist, because they have deep expertise in a particular area. Not only do they have more specialized knowledge, but they also charge more because their services are in higher demand. The same logic applies in coaching—the key to standing out is choosing a niche.

Big Fish, Small Pond

When you have a niche, you become a big fish in a small pond. Choosing a niche allows you to define your space and authority in the market. This specialization not only helps you stand out but also makes it easier to reach your target audience and grow your coaching business.

When I first started coaching, I didn't have a niche. I worked with people from all walks of life, and while I gained experience, I found myself spread thin. Over time, my niche revealed itself. My initial focus was helping expats navigate life in their new countries. Later, I provided life coaching for the LGBT community, which evolved into relationship coaching for gay men. Eventually, I also specialized in supporting entrepreneurs with their public speaking skills.

This evolution happened naturally, and the more I honed in on my niche, the easier it became to market myself. Choosing a niche doesn't mean locking yourself into a single area forever—it means focusing your attention and energy on a specific audience or problem. Over time, your niche may evolve, but starting with a clear focus helps guide your marketing efforts and business growth.

The Power of Focused Marketing

A niche simplifies your marketing. When you're clear about who you serve and the problems you solve, it becomes much easier to know where to find your clients. Ask yourself: where do people with this specific problem hang out? How can you get your offer in front of them? The clearer your niche, the more effectively you can target your marketing and find clients.

Having a niche allows you to offer tailored coaching, which clients are often willing to pay more for. People seek specialized help for specific problems, and they'll gladly invest more in a coach who understands their unique challenges. Whether you're helping entrepreneurs scale their businesses or guiding newly divorced individuals through relationship recovery, specialization makes you stand out and attract higher-paying clients.

Person-Oriented vs. Problem-Oriented Niches

There are two main types of niches: *person-oriented* and *problem-oriented*. Let's take a few moments to break down the differences.

Person-Oriented Niche

A person-oriented niche focuses on a specific type of client or demographic. This means you tailor your coaching to meet the unique needs, backgrounds, or characteristics of a particular group.

Here are some examples of person-oriented niches:

- Single moms
- Entrepreneurs
- Retirees
- Empty nesters
- Digital nomads
- Healthcare professionals

If you're offering "life coaching," having a person-oriented niche allows you to stand out because you're not just a generic life coach—you're a coach for a specific type of person.

Problem-Oriented Niche

On the other hand, a problem-oriented niche focuses on helping clients solve specific issues or challenges, regardless of their demographic background. These challenges often fall into one of three broad categories, known as the *super niches*: health, wealth, and relationships. These are the areas where people consistently invest their time, money, and energy, so specializing here can unlock huge opportunities.

Let's dive into the *super niches and* see how problem-oriented coaching works.

1. **Health.** Health-related challenges are an evergreen market. People are always investing in ways to improve their physical and mental well-being. A health-focused coaching niche can cover a wide range of issues, so the key is to specialize within the health sector.

    Examples of health-oriented coaching niches:
    - Weight management and overcoming weight loss plateaus

- Chronic pain management (e.g., arthritis, back pain)
- Stress reduction and resilience building
- Managing hormonal imbalances (e.g., thyroid, menopause, PCOS)
- Fitness coaching for people with disabilities

2. **Wealth/Career.** Wealth-related coaching often focuses on helping clients improve their financial situations or career paths. This is an area where people are willing to invest in order to see tangible results like higher earnings, better career prospects, or financial security.

   Examples of wealth/career-oriented coaching niches:
   - Career transitions for mid-career professionals
   - Financial literacy for young entrepreneurs
   - Freelance and gig economy success strategies
   - Leadership development and public speaking for executives
   - Coaching for startup founders navigating rapid growth

3. **Relationships.** Relationships are central to our well-being, and coaching in this area covers everything from romantic relationships to family dynamics. Specializing in relationship coaching means helping clients navigate specific relational challenges.

   Examples of relationship-oriented coaching niches:
   - Coaching newly divorced individuals through recovery
   - Relationship coaching for blended families
   - Marriage counseling for empty nesters
   - Support for single parents managing co-parenting challenges
   - Dating after a spouse's death

The Power of One Niche

Some coaches fall into the trap of trying to serve multiple niches. The problem with this approach is that it's like running two businesses. You'll need separate websites, separate offers, and separate marketing strategies. Essentially, you'll be splitting your time and focus.

Chasing two niches is like trying to catch two rabbits at once—you end up catching none. Instead, choose one niche and focus on it. Dedicate your energy to mastering that area before considering branching out.

You can always expand or pivot in the future, but to gain traction and grow your business, start by giving one niche your full attention.

Experimentation Is OKAY

When I got started, I had no idea what my niche should be. I started experimenting by coaching people from different walks of life. Over time, the niche became clear. As you coach people, notice which topics or challenges most excite you. This experimentation phase is valuable for discovering what truly resonates with you as a coach. Pay attention to the types of clients and problems that energize you and those that feel less engaging. Your enthusiasm for certain topics can be a strong indicator of where your true niche lies.

Often, the most fulfilling niche is one where you can offer guidance based on your own experiences and growth. It's common for coaches to end up working with a version of themselves from the past. You might find yourself drawn to coaching individuals who are facing challenges you once overcame. By supporting clients who remind you of your earlier self, you bring empathy and deep understanding to the coaching relationship, making your insights and advice even more impactful.

Abundance, Not Scarcity

Many new coaches worry that choosing a niche will limit their opportunities, but the opposite is true. By narrowing your focus, you're not shutting yourself off from opportunities—you're opening up deeper, more meaningful ones. Instead of having no niche and mildly appealing to a

wider audience, having a niche allows you to strongly appeal to a smaller audience.

Even if only 0.01 percent of the population fits into your niche, you're still set for life. Consider the vast number of English-speaking people in the world. There are over 1.5 billion English speakers globally.

1.5 billion × 0.01 percent = **150,000 potential clients**

That is more than enough to build a thriving, successful coaching business.

Having a niche simplifies your marketing, boosts your impact, and allows you to charge higher rates. Whether you choose a person-oriented or problem-oriented niche, focusing on a specific group or challenge sets you apart in an otherwise crowded field.

Don't be afraid to specialize—you'll open more doors than you ever imagined.

CHAPTER 32

When You Feel Like Nothing Is Working

I t was a chilly morning, and my heart was racing with excitement as I stood in front of an empty room, ready to deliver my very first coaching workshop. I had invested countless hours into preparing a presentation that I believed could truly change lives. In my mind, I pictured an eager audience hanging on every word I spoke. But as the minutes passed, the only thing that filled the room was silence—and the realization that no one was coming.

When the time finally came to close the session, the harsh reality hit me like a cold wave: no one showed up. The quiet was deafening, and I felt utterly exposed and vulnerable. This was not how I imagined my coaching career would begin. In that raw moment of disappointment, I questioned everything. Was I really cut out to be a coach? Was I fooling myself? It seemed like I wasn't the coach I had envisioned myself to be.

But instead of allowing myself to collapse under the weight of rejection, I felt a steady strength build inside me. A new determination rose up, stronger than ever before. I realized that I had a moral obligation to share the power of coaching because I knew firsthand how transformative it could be. This setback, as painful as it was, turned out to be the turning point that set me on my true path.

The Dual Nature of Work

When you set out to pursue your dreams, it's easy to feel disheartened when things don't go as planned. A sneaky thought can start to creep in: *nothing is working.* As a coach, you might begin to doubt your abilities when clients aren't rushing to hire you or when your income remains disappointingly low.

But work is always working. It's either working *for* you, or it's working *on* you. This is a crucial distinction that, once understood, can transform your entire perspective on the journey to success.

Think of work like a coin with two sides. When it lands on heads, it signifies that everything is going well. Clients are booking sessions, your business is growing, and things just seem to click. But when it lands on tails, it signifies challenges, obstacles, and setbacks. Here's the powerful part: when the work is working *on* you, it's shaping your character, building your skills, and pushing you toward growth in ways you might not recognize at first.

This phase of work—when things aren't going your way—is essential. During this time, you might struggle to find clients, face rejections, and wonder why your marketing efforts seem to fall flat. The offers you thought were irresistible might be met with indifference, and even scheduled calls with potential clients might fall through. It's easy in these moments to feel like nothing is working, but the truth is that *everything* is working. It's working on you, preparing you for what's ahead.

After the disastrous turnout of my first workshop, I hosted another several months later, determined to apply what I had learned. This time, I felt more prepared and confident. Yet, when the day finally arrived, only one person showed up. Instead of seeing this as another failure, I saw it as an opportunity to give everything I had to that one person. I poured my heart into the session, and by the end of it, that participant left transformed and inspired.

That's when I realized something powerful: this was the work working on me. Even though the immediate results weren't what I had hoped for, every experience was shaping me into a better coach.

The following month, when I had *two* participants, I celebrated like I had filled a stadium. My mindset shifted from "When will my business really take off?" to "This is exactly what I need right now." Every small win became a stepping stone, and I embraced the process, understanding that each challenge was essential to my growth.

Embracing the Journey

Looking back on my journey, it's clear that the setbacks I faced were some of my greatest teachers. They taught me resilience, strengthened my confidence, and prepared me for the hurdles that lay ahead. Some experiences, like rejection and failure, worked *on* me, shaping my character and mindset. Others, like small successes and wins, worked *for* me, moving me forward toward my goals.

When you embrace the full spectrum of work—the good and the challenging—you create a mindset that not only helps you achieve your goals but also enriches your life in meaningful ways. Remember, the work that happens *to* you is often more transformational than the work that happens *for* you. Those early challenges as an entrepreneur or coach force you to solve problems, take risks, and make decisions that shape who you are.

This isn't about putting a positive spin on struggle. It's about recognizing that every setback, every challenge, is happening in your best interest. Looking back, I'm grateful that my first workshop didn't have a packed audience. I'm grateful that I didn't make hundreds of thousands of dollars in my first year as a coach. Why? Because I wasn't yet the person who could handle that level of success. I needed time to grow into the coach I am today.

The work you put into your business will continue to work *on* you until you become the person capable of handling the success you desire. Every obstacle you face, every disappointment, is helping to build the skills, mindset, and resilience you need. And when the work starts working *for* you—when the clients, money, and recognition start flowing—you'll be ready to handle it with grace.

So, the next time you feel like nothing is working, take a step back. Trust that everything is working, just not in the way you might have expected. The path you're on is the one that's designed for your growth. It's shaping you into the person who can handle success not just in your business but in your life as a whole.

Every step, whether it feels like progress or a setback, is part of your evolution. Trust in the process. Trust that the work is working on you and for you.

CHAPTER 33

From Zero To One Million

T he path from zero to one million as a coach is an exciting and rewarding climb, with three distinct phases along the way. In the beginning, every dollar earned is a sign that your work matters and that people see value in what you offer. As your business expands, new opportunities open up, and each stage brings fresh ways to serve your clients and grow your impact.

What makes this process meaningful isn't just reaching financial milestones—it's seeing yourself step into a bigger vision. Every level you reach, from $0 to $10,000, $10,000 to $100,000, and $100,000 to $1 million, is a chance to deepen your skills, sharpen your focus, and build something that truly aligns with your purpose. You cannot grow a business if you do not grow the person running it, and each phase of growth invites you to evolve right alongside your business.

Here's how to build your coaching practice from the ground up, one phase at a time, until you're achieving results you once only imagined.

Phase 1:
$0 to $10,000

The jump from zero to your first dollar is the most significant step in your coaching career. It's not just about making money—it's about the mental shift that happens when you move from aspiration to action. This phase is where most aspiring coaches give up. It's crucial to recognize that, while this phase may seem the toughest, it's also the most rewarding once you break through. Here's how to navigate it:

1.   Plant Lots of Seeds

In the early stages, your number one goal is to make sure people know you're a coach. Every conversation you have is a seed planted. Even if someone doesn't hire you right away, you're building relationships, and over time, these seeds will grow into referrals and paying clients. The more seeds you plant, the greater your chances of success.

2. Go for "No"

Rejection is a natural part of the process. Don't be afraid to hear "no." The more times you hear it, the closer you are to a "yes." When you believe you can help someone, don't hesitate to invite them to hire you. When you get turned down, don't take it personally—rejection is a stepping stone to success. Embrace it as part of the journey.

3. Engage With Pro Bono Clients

In the early stages of your coaching practice, working with a few pro bono clients can be a valuable way to build confidence, gather testimonials, and refine your skills. However, it's essential to approach this strategically. Pro bono coaching should be temporary and limited to a select few clients early on.

This approach doesn't contradict the importance of charging a premium. Think of these initial pro bono clients as a launchpad—they help you build a foundation for a high-value business. Once you've gained experience and collected positive feedback, transition to charging premium rates. Pro bono work is a short-term strategy to set you up for long-term success.

Phase 2:
$10,000 to $100,000

Once you've made your first $10,000, your business is entering its adolescent phase. You've proven you can generate income; now it's time to refine your approach and scale your efforts. In this phase, you'll focus on streamlining your business, improving efficiency, and positioning yourself for growth.

1.   Grow Your Team

Hiring a virtual assistant or using software to handle routine tasks (like scheduling and invoicing) can free up your time for income-generating activities. At this stage, it's also time to consider hiring a bookkeeper or accountant to keep your finances in check. Building the right systems early on will save you time and prevent headaches later.

2.   Choose a Niche

By now, you've likely developed a sense of who your ideal clients are and what problems you're most passionate about solving. Choosing a niche allows you to become known as an expert in a specific area. This not only helps you stand out in the industry but also makes it easier to attract clients who are willing to pay for your specialized services.

3.   Pick One Channel and One Offer

Instead of spreading yourself thin with multiple offers and marketing channels, focus on perfecting one main offer and one primary channel of outreach. Whether it's social media, podcasting, or live events, double down on the strategy that has brought you the most success so far. Mastery in one area will take you much further than trying to be everywhere all at once. Simplicity is key.

Phase 3:
$100,000 to $1,000,000

This is the phase where your business begins to mature, and your efforts start to snowball. The systems you've put in place, the reputation you've built, and the work you've done all come together, allowing your income to grow at an accelerated pace. At this point, the goal is to further scale your business, streamline operations, and build long-term stability.

1. Create a High-Ticket Program

One of the fastest ways to increase revenue in this phase is by developing a high-ticket program. A high-ticket offer typically ranges from $5,000 to $15,000 and provides a deeper, more transformational experience for your clients. Design a comprehensive program that includes one-on-one coaching, group sessions, videos, manuals, and other resources. This type of offer not only boosts your revenue per client but also allows you to deliver more value and impact.

2. Improve Your Conversion Rates

Small improvements can lead to big results during this phase. Analyze your consultations and figure out how to better address potential clients' needs. By increasing your conversion rate, you can dramatically grow your business. For instance, if you conduct ten consultations a month and convert five clients at $10,000 each, that's $50,000 per month. A slight improvement in your conversion rate can exponentially increase your earnings.

3. Trim the Rosebush

As your business scales, you'll likely accumulate a lot of unnecessary processes, offers, or tasks. This is where you need to "trim the rosebush." Simplify your operations by cutting out anything that's not contributing directly to your growth. Focus on the activities that generate the most value and eliminate what's slowing you down. Trimming your processes will help you scale more efficiently and prevent burnout.

The Snowball Effect: Hitting $1,000,000

As you approach the million-dollar mark, something interesting happens: your business starts running with less effort from you. You've built systems, trained a team, and refined your processes to the point where the business becomes a self-sustaining entity. This is the ultimate goal—a business that generates income without needing you to be involved in every detail.

This is where you experience the "snowball effect." Your business not only sustains itself but begins to grow faster than ever before. You'll likely reach a point where you wake up and realize that the machine you've built is working for you, creating consistent income without as much direct input. This is a moment worth celebrating.

When you hit the million-dollar mark, you'll feel an immense sense of accomplishment. You've built a money-making machine that runs on autopilot, providing you with freedom and security. And while the journey wasn't easy, it was absolutely worth it.

Remember, success doesn't happen overnight. Every phase of your coaching journey brings new challenges and opportunities. Stay focused, keep refining your strategies, and enjoy the process. After all, this isn't just about making money—it's about building a life and business that you love.

CHAPTER 34

When To Quit Your Job And Go All-In

I f you're thinking about diving full-time into your coaching business, you're definitely not alone. This question comes up a lot, and it usually brings along its friends: nerves, doubt, and a healthy dose of "what if" scenarios. It's totally normal. But the magic only starts happening when you push past that doubt and lean into the possibilities.

I used to have a part-time job that I considered my safety net. I wasn't passionate about it, but it paid the bills—$3k a month, to be exact. It was predictable. I knew my food and rent would be covered, and I figured I could juggle my job while growing my coaching business on the side. The perfect balance, right?

Well, that balance didn't last long. A tension started to grow between me and my employer, caused by my growing lack of enthusiasm for the job and my increasing focus on building my coaching business. I could feel the scales tipping, but I didn't make a move—until the rug was pulled completely out from under me.

One day, I got the phone call: *"We have to let you go."*

The pit in my stomach opened up like a chasm. My world felt like it was collapsing in on itself. The security I had been holding onto vanished in an instant. All the "what if" scenarios I had feared rushed into my mind at once. I had no idea how I was going to get by without that $36k salary. I felt like everything I had planned for was crumbling.

But, in that heart-stopping moment, something else crept in— something unexpected. Amid the fear, there was a strange sense of liberation. I suddenly had control over my future in a way I never had before. I was standing at the edge of a cliff, and the only way forward was to jump. It was terrifying, but also thrilling. I knew I was free to shape my life in any way I wanted.

Still, my biggest fear was, *"How will I make money now?"*

That $36k from my job had felt like the bare minimum I could rely on. Then, a mentor asked me a question that shifted everything: *"What if, in a year, you make more than $36k?"*

It was a lightning bolt moment. I had been thinking way too small. A year later, I looked back in awe. I didn't just make $36k—I made nearly $100k. And here's the kicker: in just *one* of those months, I made $36k. The exact amount I used to see as my ceiling was now my floor. When you pour your energy into something you truly care about, the results can blow your mind.

Reflecting on that year, I realized something deeper was at play. In retrospect, getting fired wasn't a disaster—it was the universe giving me a loving nudge. I had already outgrown that position, but I was too scared to quit. I had been holding on to the false security of a predictable paycheck, even though my passion was pulling me in a different direction. The universe stepped in and gave me the push I needed off the edge of the diving board. I see now that I needed that moment to realize my potential. It was as if life was saying, *"You've got this—now go all in."*

Think about the energy you may currently be putting into a job you don't love. Even with the lack of passion you may likely have for that job, you have still been able to reach some level of success. Now, imagine how successful you will be when you actually put your energy into coaching—work that actually aligns with your values. The results are remarkably different.

Energy goes where attention flows. The more focus you put on a goal, the faster you will see results. If you're putting 10 percent into your coaching business and aren't happy with the results, it's no surprise. It's like expecting a six-pack by hitting the gym twice a month. This doesn't mean that you aren't capable of success.

Oftentimes, the only thing preventing you from seeing success is because you haven't really given your coaching dream a fighting chance. When you go all-in on your dreams, that's when the real magic happens. Instead of worrying things won't work out, what if you surprise yourself with what you're capable of? Imagine the kind of success you could create when you give 100 percent to your coaching business.

What if you fully committed yourself to your coaching goals for a whole year? One year to dedicate yourself to your dream without holding back. Even if you don't make a substantial amount of money, the personal growth you'll experience is worth its weight in gold.

Think of it as an experiment—a one-year trial. Remember, that the corporate world will always be there if you need to go back. You can always find another job if you need to. But what if, instead, you find a life you never want to leave?

I'm not suggesting that everyone should abruptly quit their jobs without careful consideration. However, there are signs it might be time to move on:

- You feel confident in your coaching abilities and have built some momentum with clients.
- You understand how to effectively market yourself.
- You sense that the only thing holding you back is dedicating your full attention and time to making it thrive.

Some of our students in the Thriving Coach Academy quit their jobs within just a few months into our program. Others scaled back to part-time first or found low-stress jobs to cover essentials while they built their business. You don't have to go all-in all at once if that doesn't feel right for you. This is about making a move that honors your growth, not staying small to keep others comfortable. Trust in knowing what is right for you.

One last note: if you're worried about feeling disloyal to your job or the people you've been committed to, consider this perspective: you're not betraying anyone—you're honoring your growth and evolution. We are here on this planet to grow, and growth requires adaptation. When you feel called to show up in a bigger way, you're fulfilling your evolutionary role as a human.

There's a powerful phrase: **"You're either growing or dying."**

While it's natural to worry about betraying others, don't betray yourself in the process. There are two types of people in your life: those who care about what you do for them and those who care about who you are. The ones who value who you are will celebrate and support your path forward—they're the people worth keeping close.

On the other hand, those who only care about what you do for them may feel frustrated or bothered when you choose to move on. You can leave your current role with grace and dignity by expressing genuine appreciation for the experience and relationships you've built.

You will never feel 100% prepared before you take the leap. The key lies in making the transition before you feel fully ready.

There's no perfect time to make the leap, and you don't need to wait until all your fears and doubts disappear.

As you explore your decision to go all-in with coaching, know that the only real security comes from within. You are your own safety net. It's not in a paycheck or job title—it's in the courage to bet on yourself. One year from now, you might look back and realize that the moment you let go was the moment you truly began to soar.

What if you surprise yourself with what you are capable of? Go chase that answer. The world is waiting for what only you can offer—maybe it's time to not keep it waiting any longer.

CHAPTER 35

Are Your Business Goals Too Big?

D uring one of our coaching program modules, one of my students raised a poignant question that struck a chord with many in the room:

"How do I know if I'm aiming too high, if my goals are too big?"

This question is not uncommon among aspiring coaches and ambitious individuals alike. Perhaps, like her, you wonder if you're truly capable of achieving the big dreams you hold for yourself. Maybe you second-guess whether your goals are too lofty, too far out of reach.

That question sparked a powerful conversation, one that invited everyone in the room—and perhaps you as well—to look at their dreams in a new light. What if those big goals aren't too lofty, but are calling you to grow in ways you haven't yet imagined?

Rather than holding back, you might discover that your dreams are asking you to step up and trust in your ability to make them a reality.

Your Dreams Are Not Random—They Are Made For You

The first concept to embrace is this: You wouldn't have your dreams if you weren't meant to achieve them. I'll repeat that because it's crucial. *You wouldn't have your dreams if you weren't meant to achieve them.* Your deepest desires and goals are not arbitrary—they are reflections of your potential.

Whenever you envision something greater for yourself, it's because you are already equipped with the capability to make it a reality. Those big dreams that keep tugging at your soul? They're aligned with your strengths, talents, and growth. Rather than doubting whether you're truly capable, trust that your aspirations are signals of what you're meant to pursue.

Your dreams are a reflection of the impact you're capable of making.

240

Instead of wondering, "Is my dream too big? Am I aiming too high?" shift the question to, "Why am I already the person who can make this happen?" This shift in perspective allows you to see your goals not as distant or unreachable, but as aligned with the unique strengths you already possess.

Many people I've worked with describe their calling to become a coach as sudden, random, or even scary. But upon deeper reflection, we often realize that their entire lives have been pointing them in this direction. Their experiences, skills, and interactions with others were all preparing them for this moment. Your dream to pursue coaching—or any other significant goal—did not come out of nowhere. It's aligned with the strengths you already have, even if you can't fully see it yet.

You Will Grow Into the Person Who Achieves Your Dreams

You may not feel fully equipped to achieve your dreams right now, and that's okay. The important thing to keep in mind is this: as you move toward your dreams, you naturally grow into the person who can achieve them. Your dreams are signals of where you need to focus your growth and energy.

When people doubt their ability to achieve their goals, it's often because they're focused solely on their current capabilities and circumstances. They look at where they are right now, what they currently know, and what skills they presently have. But your dreams don't expect you to have everything figured out from the start. They are part of your personal evolution. As you take action, you'll develop the necessary skills, knowledge, and resources along the way.

If you only sit with your dream, it remains just that—a dream. But if you take even small steps forward, you'll begin to discover the skills you didn't know you had, and you'll learn what you need to learn in order to achieve your goal. Your dreams are not static. They evolve as you do. The more you work toward them, the more you realize you're becoming the person you need to be to achieve them.

If you ever doubt yourself or the magnitude of your goals, remember this: Your dreams are not bigger than you. They are just big enough to challenge you to grow. Big dreams can be intimidating, and it's natural to feel fear or uncertainty. But rather than letting that fear hold you back, recognize that it's a sign you're stepping into something significant.

Your dreams are designed to stretch you, to push you to grow into the next version of yourself. They aren't there to be second-guessed or questioned—they're there to show you where you need to focus your energy.

Your Goals Are an Invitation to Leadership

Often, when people doubt whether they're truly cut out for their big dreams, it's because they're questioning their leadership ability. Maybe you've had experiences in the past where you doubted your ability to lead or where others made you question it.

Aspiring coaches and leaders have big dreams because they are meant to lead others. That's the simple truth of the matter. If the size of your goal intimidates you, that's a sign of the magnitude of the impact you're capable of making. Your dreams aren't just about you—they're about the people whose lives you're meant to touch, influence, and lead.

When you begin to see your goals as an invitation to step into leadership, it becomes a powerful motivator. Your aspirations are signals that you have something significant to offer the world, and they're also a sign that the world needs you to step up. If you're being called to be a bigger leader, to share your voice, to take up space—yes, you might feel fear, but that fear is a sign that you're on the right path.

Embracing the Fear and Moving Forward

It's natural to feel fear when you're pursuing big dreams. Fear often arises when you're stepping into the unknown, pushing beyond your comfort zone, and taking on challenges that will stretch you. But fear doesn't mean you're on the wrong path. In fact, it's often a sign that you're exactly where you need to be.

The key is to embrace the fear and keep moving forward. Don't let it paralyze you or convince you that your dreams are too big or unattainable. Instead, see it as part of the process of growth and transformation. The fear is simply a sign that you're stepping into a new level of leadership, purpose, and potential.

Your dreams are not random. They are reflections of your potential and signals of the impact you're meant to make. As you pursue them, you will naturally grow into the person who can achieve them. They aren't too big for you—they're just big enough to challenge you to grow and lead.

When doubt creeps in, remember: your dreams are just right. They are not bigger than you, and they are calling you to step into the next phase of your leadership and personal growth. By moving forward through fear, you become the person capable of living the life you desire.

"I had a huge life event that made me rethink what I wanted to bring to my life. As soon as I pictured myself coaching, I knew this was it. I currently work as a senior level manager at a global company. The last twenty years, I've grown a lot, but I knew this wasn't my final destination. I wanted something different. Serving others was that missing piece. I knew I was destined for something else. Since enrolling in Thriving Coach Academy, seeing the impact to the clients that I've already been able to create has been huge. Within a few months, I enrolled my three paying clients. The timeline has been surprising. My wife and I have five kids, so the flexibility of time and location independence this business allows is a huge benefit for me.

If you're somebody who is considering a career in coaching, you may have a fear of starting, like I did. You may downplay your ability to be successful and overvalue the status quo. Looking back from where I am now, I realize your ability to be successful is exponential. The cost of the status quo is really high. My advice for students is to know that you have your own uniqueness. We all have very different backgrounds, styles, and personalities, and it all works. We're all gonna have different clients who are drawn to us. Instead of comparing yourself too much to others, recognize that your gifts are unique."

- YAMATO Y.

TOP 10 INSIGHTS

1. Your clients are closer than you think, often waiting in unexpected places, ready to hire you.

2. Your unique essence, vibe, and story will naturally attract the people who are meant to work with you.

3. You don't have to market yourself everywhere—focus on one strategy that resonates with you and aligns with your strengths, and you can still achieve massive success.

4. With a Premium Business Model, you gain freedom by working with fewer high-ticket clients while making a significant impact on their lives.

5. Choosing a niche helps you stand out as a specialist, enabling you to become a big fish in a small pond and attract more clients.

6. Even when it feels like nothing is working, every experience is shaping you into the coach you're meant to be.

7. As your business grows, so does your leadership, and over time, your business will snowball and run on its own.

8. You'll never feel 100% ready to go all-in, but betting on yourself and taking action is how you create success.

9. Redirecting the energy you've been putting into a job you don't love can create incredible momentum in your coaching business.

10. Your dreams are a reflection of your potential—they wouldn't exist if you weren't capable of achieving them.

Permission Granted

Sometimes, we are called to certain things without fully understanding why. We feel an inner nudge that beckons us toward a path both exciting and daunting. These moments of calling are often shrouded in mystery, leaving us questioning their significance. Yet, it is in these very moments that our true purpose begins to unfold.

When we have an exciting opportunity, there is sometimes a part of our mind that hesitates. It's when your brain asks you, "Is it okay to actually do this? Am I actually going to transform lives and become a coach?" It's as if we are secretly waiting for someone to grant us that final permission before we move forward. But what if I told you that the only permission you need is your own? This is your time to give yourself the green light.

From a young age, we are conditioned to seek out approval. Whether it's from parents, teachers, or peers, we learn to value their opinions over our own. This external validation becomes a crutch, and we start to believe that our dreams are only valid if they are endorsed by others. But this is a myth. The truth is, you have the power to validate your own dreams.

The thing about our dreams is that they do not leave us alone. Either we honor them and let them guide us to fulfillment, or we suppress them and live with a nagging sense of what could have been. Dreams are persistent; they are the whispers of our soul urging us to become who we are meant to be. Ignoring them leads to regret, while embracing them brings joy and purpose.

In fact, Bronnie Ware, a palliative care nurse, spent years with people in their final days and discovered a powerful truth: the most common regret of the dying is, "I wish I had the courage to live a life true to myself, not the life others expected of me." This regret is a stark reminder that time is precious and that living for others' expectations robs us of the fulfillment we crave.

The lesson here is clear: **the life you want is the life you are meant to live.**

Following your calling isn't just about personal achievement—it's about avoiding the deeper pain of never having tried at all. You don't need anyone else's approval to pursue your passions for coaching and making a difference in the world.

Granting yourself permission to pursue your calling is a liberating act of self-respect.

It's an acknowledgment that you are worthy of pursuing your dreams and that your aspirations are valid. When you give yourself the green light, you become the author of your own story, rather than a character waiting for someone else to write your next chapter.

We only have one life to live. Every moment you spend waiting for permission is a moment lost. Life is happening now, and it is up to you to seize the opportunities before you. You deserve to experience the joy of seeing your clients thrive, to feel the fulfillment that comes from making a significant impact, and to enjoy the financial and personal freedom that a successful coaching career can bring.

You read this book for a reason. Something within you resonated with the message, a spark was ignited, and a vision for your future began to take shape. This book has guided you on a journey of self-discovery and growth, preparing you to step into your role as a coach. Now, it's time to act on what you've learned.

Your clients are waiting for someone just like you to step up. The world is waiting for you to say yes to yourself. Picture yourself running a coaching business you love. See the faces of your clients light up as they achieve breakthroughs and overcome challenges. Feel the sense of fulfillment and joy that comes from knowing you are making a real difference in their lives. This is not a distant dream; it is a reality that you can create. All it takes is giving yourself permission to begin.

You already have a unique set of skills, experiences, and perspectives to bring to the table. These are your gifts, and they are what will set you apart from everyone else. Embrace them. Your journey has equipped you with the tools you need to succeed. You don't have to be perfect; you just have to be willing to start.

This is more than just a goal—it's a moral obligation. If you know you are called to share your gifts, and you decide to withhold them, then it is a disservice to the world. Not sharing your talents is like hiding a light under a bushel, depriving others of the illumination and inspiration they need. You have a responsibility to share your gifts because they have the power to transform lives.

Not everyone receives this nudge to show up in a bigger way. The fact that you received that nudge is evidence that you have something special inside, and there are people out there waiting to be transformed by your support. When you realize you have the ability to help, it becomes an invitation to share your gifts with others. Accept that invitation.

It starts with giving yourself permission to take that first step. As you reach the end of this book, take a moment to reflect on the journey you have been on. Recognize the growth, the insights, and the shifts that have brought you to this point. You have everything you need to succeed as a coach and to make a profound difference in the lives of others.

The only thing left is to recognize yourself as the permission slip you've been waiting for. You have permission to pursue your dreams. You have permission to become a coach. You have permission to make a huge difference in the world and to transform lives.

It is your birthright to shine, take up space, and enjoy the abundance the world has to offer. You are worth every bit of success and happiness that comes your way. The world is ready for you to shine. Your clients are waiting for you. The time to act is now. Permission granted.

Congratulations!

Your journey into the world of coaching is important, and I'm honored to have played a role in it.

If you've found value in these pages, I'd deeply appreciate it if you could leave a review. Your feedback not only supports me but also helps others discover this book and start their own coaching journeys.

As you continue your path, I want to invite you to take the next step by enrolling in **Thriving Coach Academy**. Our program is designed to support you with the implementation of this book—from mastering the art of coaching to building and running a successful coaching business.

To learn more about our curriculum, scan the QR code below, or go to **www.thrivingcoachacademy.com**.

Thank you again for your time, dedication, and passion for making a difference. Your journey is just beginning, and I can't wait to see the incredible impact you'll make as a coach.

The Coaching Wealth Blueprint

The following section reveals the paths to hitting varying levels of income as a coach. I'll help you visualize how to reach these income goals, even if math isn't your strong suit. You'll see how you can create a great living for yourself, even with a small, focused client base.

Before diving into the numbers, take a moment to reflect on what you would love to earn as a coach. Many people don't even consider this question, but it's essential to declare your goals and desires. Would you love to earn $10,000 per month, or perhaps more?

Whatever your number is, say it out loud. Even if there are people around, boldly declare what you would love to earn as a coach. Say it a few more times, until it does not feel as awkward. The first time I said that I wanted to make $10,000 per month as a coach, I felt like I was saying something that could get me in trouble—almost like I was saying a bad word. It felt intimidating at first, but the more I thought about it, the more achievable it became.

Imagine what it would be like to be consistently making that amount you declared every month. What difference would it make for you and your loved ones? Maybe you would take that dream vacation, buy a new home, pay off debts, or simply enjoy financial freedom and peace of mind.

That's all possible for you once you have the right formula. Let's break down the exact math behind how you will build a thriving coaching business.

Income Levels and Program Types

$100 to $500 Program. This is considered a low-ticket offer, which is usually an introductory coaching program or entry-level group coaching experience. It's possible that your clients may begin with this offer before investing in one of your higher tier offers.

$1,000 to $2,500 Program. These are considered mid-ticket offer offers, which generally include some degree of one-on-one coaching. With these programs, clients receive more personalized attention and tailored guidance.

$5,000 or $10,000 Program. These are considered high-ticket offers, usually VIP one-on-one coaching or a robust and comprehensive coaching program. This offers your clients the deepest level of value and transformation.

You do not need to have offers at every price point. In most cases, you will have only one or two signature offers for a client to invest in. When you're first starting out, you may enroll clients at a lower price point—often in the $100 to $500 range—since this allows clients to get a taste of your coaching.

As you gain experience and start accumulating testimonials, you'll find that it becomes easier to attract clients and that demand for your services increases. With this growing confidence and proven value, you'll likely feel comfortable raising your rates and offering more comprehensive, higher-ticket programs. This gradual approach lets you build a sustainable coaching practice while expanding both your impact and income over time.

Income Goal: $5,000 Per Month

Number of Clients	Price of Your Program	Total Income
5 Clients	$1,000 Program	$5,000
2 Clients	$2,500 Program	$5,000
1 Client	$5,000 Program	$5,000

Income Goal: $10,000 Per Month

10 Clients	$1,000 Program	$10,000
4 Clients	$2,500 Program	$10,000
2 Clients	$5,000 Program	$10,000

Income Goal: $20,000 Per Month

8 Clients	$2,500 Program	$20,000
4 Clients	$5,000 Program	$20,000
2 Clients	$10,000 Program	$20,000

You don't need to be a "numbers person" to succeed in business. With simple math and a clear strategy, you can reach your financial goals and build a thriving coaching business. You can also tailor the money path to align with what you truly want—these examples are just starting points to help you see the possibilities. Hopefully, they inspire you to piece together the unique path that makes your business work for you.

In addition to money math, it's important to have a winning mindset. The thoughts you hold about yourself, your value, and your business play a role in your success. There are two kinds of thoughts you can have when it comes to your coaching business. Zero Dollar Thoughts are thoughts that *repel* clients, money, and opportunities. Million Dollar Thoughts *attract* clients, money, and opportunities.

Zero Dollar Thoughts often bring up emotions like anxiety, doubt, shame, guilt, confusion, and impatience, leading to procrastination, self-comparison, and a lack of investment in your business. For my first year as a coach, I had just about every Zero Dollar Thought you can imagine. It was not until I took responsibility for my attitude that I started to feel more enthusiastic about my path forward as a coach.

To save you the time, here is a collection of thoughts that have supported me in reaching my first million as a coach. Consider "trying on" these thoughts for yourself, just as you would try on clothes. Trying on a thought means to experiment with it, see how it feels, and notice how it influences your actions and emotions.

Here are some Zero Dollar Thoughts that will not serve you:

Zero Dollar Thoughts

- I'm a bad coach.
- I'm not a real professional.
- I'm not ready to put myself out there.
- I don't know where to find clients.
- No one wants what I have to offer.
- No one can afford my coaching.
- People's problems are too big for me to coach them.
- I'm wasting my time with all this.
- If I take someone's money, I am making their life worse.
- I am desperate for clients.
- I'm not disciplined or focused enough.
- I'm not experienced enough.
- I'm not smart enough to succeed.
- I'm not tech savvy.
- I'm too shy or introverted to network.
- I'm too young/old to do this.
- I'm not worth people's time.

In contrast, Million Dollar Thoughts are beliefs that drive you toward success. These thoughts create feelings of calm, certainty, clarity, excitement, patience, and determination. When you embrace these thoughts, you attract clients, put yourself out there, share your voice, connect with people, invest back into your business, and allow yourself to receive support.

Million Dollar Thoughts

- I have something unique and valuable to offer.
- I am confident in my abilities.
- I'm the right coach for the people I meet.
- I know that I can help people.
- Finding clients is simple and fun.
- My clients are waiting for me.
- Every action I take is moving me forward.
- Everything is unfolding perfectly.
- People want to pay me.
- My clients feel like they hit the jackpot when they work with me.
- The amount of value that I create will come back to me tenfold.
- When my clients pay me, their lives get significantly better.
- Success is my natural state.
- I am worthy of financial abundance.
- I deserve success and happiness.
- I am destined for greatness.
- I am unstoppable.

By adopting these Million Dollar Thoughts, you will proceed as if your success is inevitable—the best way to show up to any goal in life. When you truly believe in your success, you act in ways that make it a reality. Your confidence, determination, and positive energy will attract opportunities, resources, and support, making your success inevitable.

ABOUT THE AUTHOR

Frank Macri is the Founder of *Thriving Coach Academy* and the host of the *Life Coaching Secrets* podcast. With over a decade of experience, Macri has become a leading authority on helping individuals unlock their potential and create lucrative coaching careers.

As the creator of The Rulebook Coaching Method™, Macri has guided thousands of coaches to achieve profound breakthroughs in their sessions. He specializes in supporting coaches offering high-ticket packages, using marketing strategies that prioritize value and authentic relationships.

In this book, Macri shares his roadmap for creating a sustainable coaching career, including how he earned his first million. Outside of coaching, he enjoys tennis, board games, and time with his dog, Chai.

Made in the USA
Columbia, SC
28 April 2025

57228392R00152